DAVID BUSCH'S POINT-AND-SHOOT

COMPACT FIELD GUIDE

David D. Busch | Dan Simon

Course Technology PTR
A part of Cengage Learning

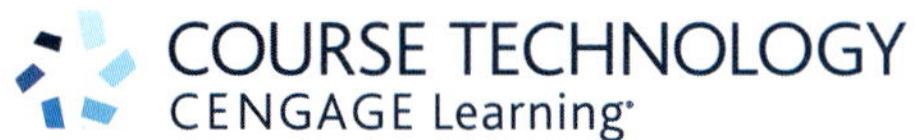

Australia, Brazil, Japan, Korea, Mexico, Singapore, Spain, United Kingdom, United States

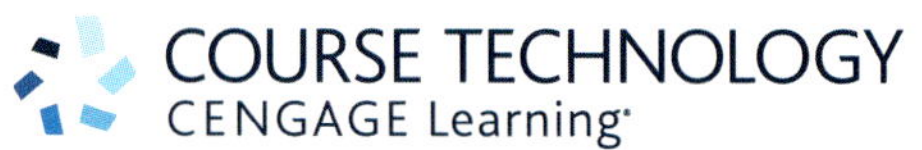

David Busch's Point-and-Shoot Compact Field Guide
David D. Busch, Dan Simon

Publisher and General Manager, Course Technology PTR:
Stacy L. Hiquet

Associate Director of Marketing:
Sarah Panella

Manager of Editorial Services:
Heather Talbot

Senior Marketing Manager:
Mark Hughes

Executive Editor:
Kevin Harreld

Project Editor:
Jenny Davidson

Series Technical Editor:
Michael D. Sullivan

Interior Layout Tech:
Bill Hartman

Cover Designer:
Mike Tanamachi

Indexer:
Katherine Stimson

Proofreader:
Sara Gullion

For product information and technology assistance, contact us at **Cengage Learning Customer & Sales Support, 1-800-354-9706.**

For permission to use material from this text or product, submit all requests online at **cengage.com/permissions**. Further permissions questions can be e-mailed to **permissionrequest@cengage.com**.

Library of Congress Control Number: 2012934303

ISBN-13: 978-1-133-59740-7

ISBN-10: 1-133-59740-8

Cengage Learning is a leading provider of customized learning solutions with office locations around the globe, including Singapore, the United Kingdom, Australia, Mexico, Brazil, and Japan. Locate your local office at: **international.cengage.com/region**.

Cengage Learning products are represented in Canada by Nelson Education, Ltd.

For your lifelong learning solutions, visit **courseptr.com**.

Visit our corporate Web site at **cengage.com**.

Printed in the United States of America
1 2 3 4 5 6 7 15 14 13

Contents

Introduction

If you're ready to graduate from point-and-shoot photography to *think*-and-shoot creativity, this book will help you put the amazing features hidden inside even the most humble snapshot camera to work. Do you wish you had the most essential information you need to shoot compelling candid portraits, amazing landscape and travel shots, or eye-opening close-ups? Perhaps you want to capture kids or grandkids playing sports, or snap better photos of your pets. We've condensed the basic material you need to upgrade your pixel skills in this handy, lay-flat book, *David Busch's Point-and-Shoot Compact Field Guide.* In it, you'll find the explanations of *why* to use each of your camera's capabilities to capture great photos of family, friends, or any subjects you want to photograph. That's the kind of information that is missing from the cheat-sheets and the book packaged with your camera. Everything in this book is written to help you out in the field, as a quick reference you can refer to as you master the full range of things your compact digital camera can do.

About the Authors

Dan Simon is an adjunct professor in the Culture and Communications Department at the College of Arts and Sciences at Drexel University. He teaches courses on a wide variety of topics, including online journalism, fundamentals of journalism, public relations, public speaking, desktop publishing, business and technical communications, and communication theory. He has also taught courses in camera techniques and digital photography for East Stroudsburg University and desktop publishing for Gloucester County College.

Dan also has more than 30 years of experience as a writer and photographer. He is currently working on a doctorate in culture and communication at Drexel University. His published works include the *Digital Photography Bible Desktop Edition* (John Wiley and Sons Publishing), *Digital Photography All-in-One* (Wiley), and *Digital Photos, Movies, & Music Gigabook for Dummies* (Wiley). He is also a regular contributor to the *Growing Edge Magazine* (hydroponics) and *Pennsylvania Magazine* (regional, travel).

He began his career as a Navy journalist with assignments aboard several ships, and in Norfolk, Va.; Dededo, Guam; and McMurdo Station, Antarctica. He has traveled to all seven continents and photographed many of America's scenic and wild places. Dan also serves as a guest photography lecturer for Norwegian Cruise Line, the Delta Queen Steamboat Company, and Royal Caribbean International.

With more than a million books in print, **David D. Busch** is the world's #1 selling digital camera guide author, and the originator of popular digital photography series like *David Busch's Pro Secrets, David Busch's Quick Snap Guides,* and *David Busch's Guides to Digital SLR Photography.* As a roving photojournalist for more than 20 years, he illustrated his books, magazine articles, and newspaper reports with award-winning images. Busch operated his own commercial studio, suffocated in formal dress while shooting weddings-for-hire, and shot sports for a daily newspaper and upstate New York college. His photos and articles have appeared in *Popular Photography, Rangefinder, Professional Photographer*, and hundreds of other publications. He's also reviewed dozens of digital cameras for CNet and other Ziff-Davis publications, and his advice has been featured on NPR's *All Tech Considered.*

Visit his website at www.dslrguides.com/blog.

Chapter 1

Your Point-and-Shoot Camera

Although smart phones with lots of megapixels (*high resolution*) have become ubiquitous, there are plenty of reasons why point-and-shoot cameras are growing in popularity. While many are the same size and weight as a smart phone (and many more are even *smaller*), there are lots of things you can do with a point-and-shoot camera that you can't do with a camera phone, and many more things that you can do with both, but which are a lot more convenient with an honest-to-gosh camera.

Here are some advantages of the typical point-and-shoot camera:

- **More zoom.** Virtually every point-and-shoot model has a nifty zoom lens that lets you magnify your subject a minimum of 3X, and often 10X, 20X, or more. And those zoom ratios count only high-quality *optical* zoom, which uses shifting lens elements to magnify the image in a way that maintains image quality. *Digital zoom,* found in camera phones (and as an option with point-and-shoot cameras, too), enlarges the picture by making the final pixels bigger, which reduces quality.
- **Wider/Longer.** While point-and-shoot models have a larger range of magnification in an absolute sense, they also usually provide views that are much wider (to take in more scenery, say) or longer range (to bring your kid's championship-winning score that much closer).
- **Better in low light.** Point-and-shoot cameras often have lenses that are able to capture more light, and sensors that respond better to low light levels, allowing you to take pictures under dimmer conditions—without annoying flash.
- **Annoying flash.** Many camera phones have an LED next to the lens that can emit a burst of light to fill in dark shadows when absolutely necessary. Most point-and-shoot cameras have a more robust non-LED electronic flash unit that does a better job for those times when you need that "annoying" flash to get the picture at all.

- **"Unlimited" storage.** Your camera phone probably has 16GB, 32GB, or 64GB of internal memory for storage of your pictures. When you consider that this memory is shared with all your apps, videos, and other data, that may not be a lot, especially on a long trip. While a few camera phones accept removable memory cards, virtually all point-and-shoot cameras (with only a few exceptions) have a slot where you can quickly replace a full card with a fresh, empty one, in seconds. (See Figure 1.1.)
- **More features and accessories.** Camera phones have a limited number of special features. Depending on your model, point-and-shoot cameras may have cool double exposure capabilities, GPS tagging of your photos, super-high shutter speeds, and facial recognition to find and label images of your friends (as you shoot). You can often buy add-on lens and filter accessories that are much more versatile than those offered for camera phones, and the very latest models use the Android operating system (similar to that used on many smart phones) so you can download and run interesting apps right on your camera.

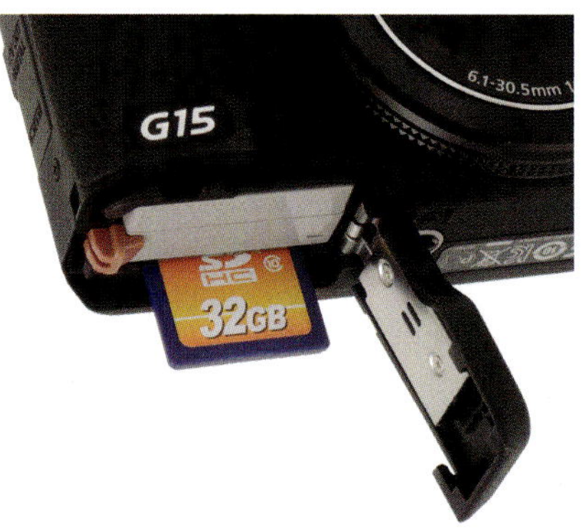

Figure 1.1
Point-and-shoot cameras have virtually unlimited storage space.

The range of available point-and-shoot cameras is very large, from models barely larger than a stack of credit cards, priced at less than $100, to sophisticated cameras that are used primarily in point-and-shoot mode, but which have interchangeable lenses and optional manual controls. These higher-end models can easily cost $500, and some threaten to nudge the $1,000 price point. This large variety of types stems from the broad spectrum of users, all of whom want a camera that they can point-and-click when they want to capture the moment, but with the option to point-and-think when that moment is ripe for some creativity.

You'll find point-and-shoot cameras toted by non-photographers who want more than their camera phone can give them; by beginners who are blossoming into avid photographers; and by enthusiasts who want a real camera they can carry with them at all times. They are also popular among advanced photographers—both amateur and pro—who want a "walk-about" camera for those times when they don't want to carry their heavier gear (or who need an emergency back-up). This chapter will help you sort out the key factors in choosing a point-and-shoot that suits your needs.

What's Important/What's Not?

Take an inventory of the capabilities you need from a camera. If you're going to be doing a lot of sports, nature, or child photography, a responsive camera with minimal shutter lag (that delay between when you press the shutter button and when the camera actually takes the picture) is important. Also key are fast and automatic focus to lock in on your subject, and rapid shooting so you can capture a sequence of events as it unfolds. On the other hand, if you're photographing a lot of school plays and performances, you might need a camera that works well in low light and has a "quiet" mode so you don't disturb the performers. If you frequently make enlargements of your vacation pictures for display in your home, you might want a camera with many megapixels so your blow-ups can be as sharp and clear as any smaller prints you make, or the images you view on your computer screen.

But when examining features, keep in mind that many of the bells and whistles advertised for these cameras are there more to convince you that you need an upgrade and to buy a new camera, than for any photographic reason. While there are some legitimate features, such as easy panoramas, high-definition video, or HDR (high dynamic range photography, to capture detail in both the brightest highlights and deepest shadows), there are also gimmicks that have little benefit to your photography, such as playing MP3 audio files or providing a "digital zoom." Your smart phone can do that—you expect more from your point-and-shoot. Even when features do have value in general, the question to ask is "Do they have any value to me?" The most important considerations when buying a point-and-shoot camera include ease of use, durability, and compatibility.

Megapixels—or Other Concerns?

One of the biggest yet least important questions camera buyers worry about is how many megapixels their camera sensor contains. The irony is that unless you actually do get enlargements printed, almost any resolution camera will do the job. If you do regularly have prints made from your digital images, a 10-megapixel camera will give you more than enough resolution to get even large (16 × 20 inches or bigger) prints made. We'll talk a bit more about resolution a little later in this field guide, but resolution doesn't have to be your main concern in shopping for a digital camera. Instead, consider the following features:

- **Optical zoom.** The greater the range of the camera's optical zoom, the greater the variety of shooting situations you can handle. The term "optical" zoom can be thought of as the camera's "real" zoom, unmagnified by any digital tricks. This is the more important consideration when you see a camera advertisement that mentions both the "optical" and the "digital" zoom. Cameras with 20:1 (20X) and even greater zoom ranges are easy to find these days. Give greater weight to cameras that offer these longer zoom ranges using optical technology only.
- **Versatile sensor sensitivity.** The camera's sensitivity (ISO) setting controls how responsive the camera is to light. The higher the ISO number, the greater the sensitivity, allowing you to keep shooting in low light conditions. Keep in mind, the higher the ISO is set, the poorer the relative quality of the image. ISO 100-200 provides the best quality for shooting in daylight. ISO settings of 400-800 might be best for sports, and higher values for low light. Many point-and-shoot cameras offer ISO settings from 64 to 6400 or greater. While you'll want to stick to the lowest ISO setting appropriate for your scene, it's nice to have a range of settings to choose from.
- **Continuous shooting mode.** Most point-and-shoot cameras offer a continuous shooting mode that lets you press and hold the shutter so the camera keeps taking pictures as long as the button is held down. Low-end cameras generally offer modest rates around one or two frames a second. Many point-and-shoot cameras offer five frames per second or better. Some higher-end point-and-shoot models with interchangeable lenses can shoot at rates of 8 to 10 fps (and up).
- **Image stabilization.** This feature helps you keep the camera steadier while shooting by allowing the sensor itself or elements in the lens to shift in sync with your camera's jitter. This is an important asset when trying to make sharp images, particularly since holding the camera at arm's length makes blur from camera shake more likely. Image stabilization won't "freeze" moving subjects, but it does a good job of reducing or eliminating blur caused by a moving camera.
- **In-camera editing.** While your camera will never replace a laptop or desktop computer loaded with Photoshop Elements or some other image-editing program, your camera can now perform many basic image-editing functions. You can trim, crop, adjust colors, improve the image tones, or

add special effects right in the camera. This can save you time and hassle later, but more importantly, this means you can often tweak your photos and then print or email them while you're still on vacation.

- **High-definition video.** Point-and-shoot cameras have had the capability of shooting VHS quality video for many years. (Many of you may have never seen a videocassette recorder, I admit.) Today, virtually all point-and-shoot models can capture standard high definition (1280 × 720 pixels, or 720p) video and/or full high definition (1920 × 1080, or 1080i/p) video. Video may not be very important to you; if so, don't be afraid of a camera that doesn't offer high quality video recording. Still, if you have any interest in video, good quality point-and-shoot cameras are capable of excellent quality video these days, often using built-in stereo microphones. You can easily get by with one of these cameras and skip the separate video camcorder if you want.
- **Articulated LCD/Touch screens.** Articulated LCD screens are useful because they let you view the image when holding the camera at arm's length at different positions, or at waist-level or held overhead. Touch screens offer a more intuitive option for operating camera controls simply by tapping on or swiping the screen, and can result in speeding up the shooting process. (See Figure 1.2.)

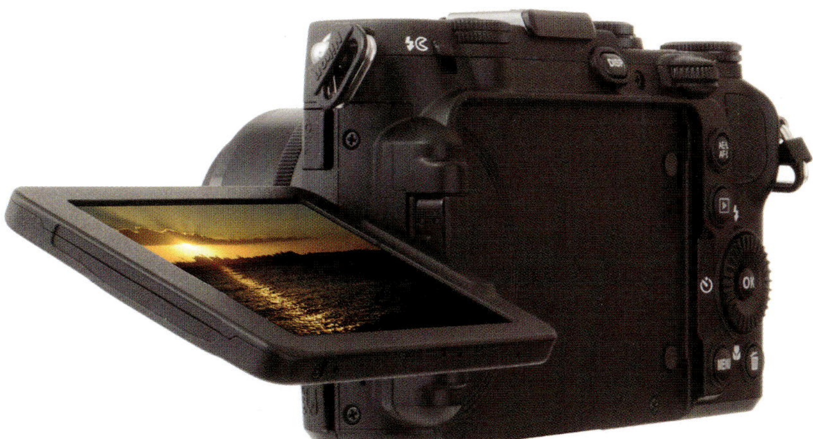

Figure 1.2 Many point-and-shoot cameras offer an articulated LCD screen that can be maneuvered as needed. Some even include a touch sensitive screen, making it possible to set many camera controls without resorting to pushing buttons or turning dials.

Types of Point-and-Shoot Cameras

Point-and-shoot cameras come in many shapes and styles. (See Figure 1.3.) Once upon a time, cameras had to be designed around a strip of film, limiting camera maker's design options. Today the camera only needs to be designed around its lens, memory card, and power source, options offering much greater flexibility.

This has led to a wide variety of choices for photo enthusiasts, ranging from small slim cameras to mini "dSLR-like" devices. Although there's no standard designation system for categorizing point-and-shoot types, we can still group these cameras into some different styles:

- **Slim and pocketable.** This class offers small and stylish cameras that can fit into a shirt pocket. While small, these cameras can be very versatile and boost serious resolution sensors.
- **Advanced point-and-shoot cameras.** While these are also small, sometimes pocketable cameras, they often feature ultra-sophisticated options rivaling those in dSLRs. They're also often the choice of pro photographers when they don't need to carry their working cameras. It's not unusual for these cameras to be able to use some of the accessories designed for their pro dSLR brethren, such as external electronic flash units or filters.
- **Mega zoom/Bridge cameras.** This style of camera resembles a shrunken dSLR. Acting as a "bridge" from the point-and-shoot to the dSLR, one of the key features these cameras offer is powerful zoom capabilities often exceeding a 20X zoom ratio or greater. Full featured and loaded with bells

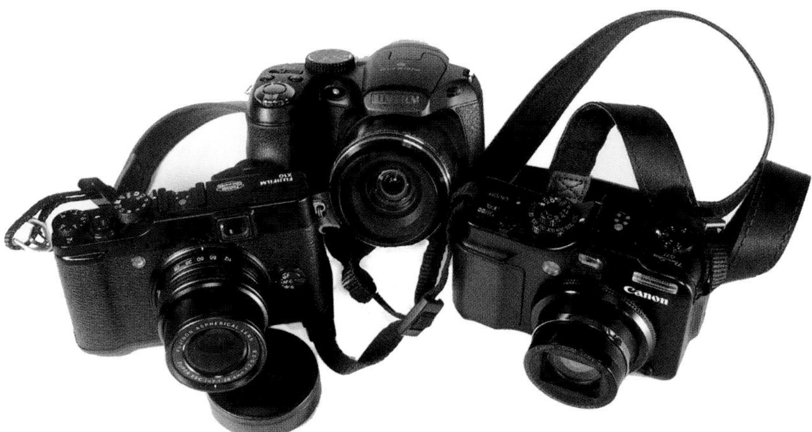

Figure 1.3 Point-and-shoot cameras come in a variety of styles and price ranges.

and whistles, many of these cameras can do it all while remaining small enough to carry comfortably.

- **"Retro" cameras.** I don't know if this is an actual technical class, but it's certainly a design class. These cameras often copy classic film camera designs or capture the spirit of older styles in general. Some of these point-and-shoot cameras are simply decent picture makers while others are incredibly powerful (and expensive) full-featured products.

Camera Buying Considerations—Price Ranges

It would take an entire book just to list all the point-and-shoot camera options on the market these days, and by the time the book came out, there would be even more models that hadn't been covered. Because price is a major concern for many camera buyers, I'm going to break this down into modestly priced, mid-range, and high-end cameras and provide a few examples of each. I'll also provide a breakdown of what separates each level by capabilities, so you'll have an idea of what you're getting or giving up.

Modestly Priced Options (under $200)

If you're shopping for a camera these days, you can look forward to more capable cameras at lower prices. If you need to get the most bang for your buck, you can look for a camera that is one model behind the most recent offering since these are often discounted once a newer model comes out. Since camera makers are releasing new models multiple times a year, your chances of saving some money this way are good.

While cameras in this price range may not be the toughest, or feature the widest variety of features, they can be decent performers. Many boast upwards of 10 megapixels and a few even fall into the bridge camera range. For the most part though, they tend to fall into the small and slim group, aimed more at less dedicated photographers. Some examples of this category include:

- **Nikon Coolpix.** Models in this line can be found for less than $200 and offer up to a 7X optical zoom. They are small and slim style cameras that can fit in a pocket and be ready to shoot quickly.
- **Panasonic Lumix.** Another slim style popular brand of camera, models start with around 12 megapixels of resolution or more and can feature Leica DC Vario-Elmar optical zooms.
- **Fujifilm FinePix.** The Fujifilm line includes "bridge" style cameras with up to 18X optical zoom and 14-megapixel or better sensors. They also shoot HD video and include a nifty, ultra simple panoramic feature that makes creating great panoramic photos easy. The typical FinePix camera also offers image stabilization.

Mid-range Options ($200–$500)

While $500 won't go all that far in buying a dSLR these days, spending between $200 and $500 can get you a very capable point-and-shoot camera. Cameras in this price range offer better construction and durability, faster, higher-quality lenses, and more features than their modestly priced brethren. They may also offer newer and superior sensors.

Some examples of this category include (see Figure 1.4):

- **Pentax Optio.** No fear of the elements with Pentax's waterproof, shockproof, crushproof, coldproof, and dustproof cameras, such as the Optio WG1. They include features like geo-tagging for your photos so you know exactly where you were when you shot them. Even if you can't fit some of the larger models into your pocket, you can always clip it to your belt with an included carabiner.
- **Canon PowerShot.** Canon has a line of compact, slim style camera PowerShots, with 12 megapixels or more of resolution, and Leica DC Vario-Elmar optical zooms.
- **Canon PowerShot G-series.** These cameras may have articulating LCD screens and improved low-light performance. The recent PowerShot G15 is a good example of the "extras" a top-grade point-and-shoot camera can offer. Besides being a very capable performer in its own right, the G15 can take advantage of some of Canon's pro dSLR accessories such as the add-on external flash units.
- **Nikon P-series.** Nikon's answer to the Canon G-series is its Coolpix 7xxx models. The latest versions added a second control dial, and feature a longer zoom lens than available with any PowerShot in Canon's G-series lineup. It also has full HD video shooting.

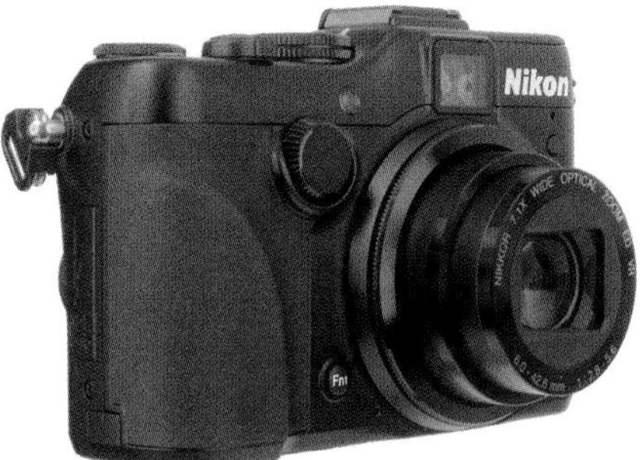

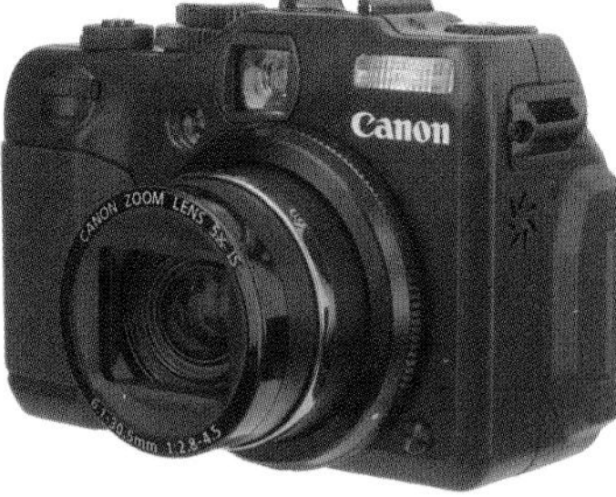

Figure 1.4 Many pros find the Nikon P-series (left) and Canon G-series cameras (right) acceptable substitutes for their high-end cameras when they just want a small camera for non-work photography.

High-end Options ($500 and Up)

When you start looking at top-of-the-line point-and-shoot cameras, you're often looking at cameras that rival dSLRs (digital single lens reflex cameras) in prices and capabilities (with the exception of interchangeable lenses). If all you look at is price tag versus capabilities, it might seem like anytime you have to choose between similarly priced point-and-shoot and dSLRs, it's a no-brainer; the greater capabilities of the dSLR make it the better choice. This misses an important fact though. Often the point-and-shoot is the more convenient, easier to use camera. When you just want to grab a camera, stick it in your pocket, and grab some photos while you're having fun, the point-and-shoot is much more desirable.

What does it take to make a top-of-the-line point-and-shoot camera these days? Solid construction, the latest greatest sensor technology, better autofocus, RAW+JPEG, super-fast premium optics, and dSLR-like control of fundamental camera settings are some of the things I expect from these premium cameras. Once the price starts climbing above $1,000, I also expect to see amazing styling and an imaging sensor comparable to the ones found in dSLRs.

Some examples of this category include:

- **Sigma DP series.** These Sigma offerings boast excellent daylight image quality from a 14.1MP Foveon sensor and fast 2.8 fixed 41mm lens.
- **Leica V-Lux series.** This Leica point-and-shoot offers a 16X optical zoom, 1080i full HD movie recording, 10 fps continuous shooting at full 14.1MP resolution, built-in GPS, and the ability to generate 3D images. The V-Lux is small enough to fit in a pocket thanks to its collapsing zoom lens.
- **Fujifilm FinePix X series.** The recent X10 model is a high-end sleek black camera that is solidly built, features a fast f/2 to f/2.8 zoom lens with the equivalent of a 28-112mm lens. Its imaging sensor creates 12MP images, but when you're dealing with difficult lighting conditions, can give you high-dynamic range 6MP files. (See Figure 1.5.)
- **Canon PowerShot G X series.** Canon's expensive ($800) G1 X is an impressive point-and-shoot camera with a sensor that is much larger than that found in most models in this class. This slightly bulkier point-and-shoot camera's jumbo sensor (virtually the same size as the sensor found in most digital SLRs), gives it the potential of better image quality. It has improved high ISO performance, but otherwise, its features are very similar to the earlier PowerShot G models. (See Figure 1.6.)

- **Olympus PEN series.** Several models of the Olympus PEN cameras are offered, and the lower-end cameras are definitely aimed at the point-and-shoot crowd. However, all of them use interchangeable Micro Four Thirds lenses (like the Olympus OM-D E-M5 described later), so they have a lot in common with other ILC (interchangeable lens camera) models.

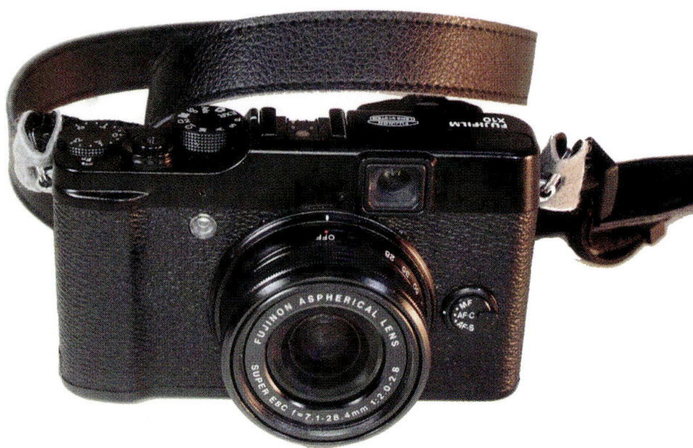

Figure 1.5
The Fujifilm FinePix X10 offers a 12MP sensor, which can react to extreme lighting conditions to produce good quality images by sacrificing pixels to increase dynamic range.

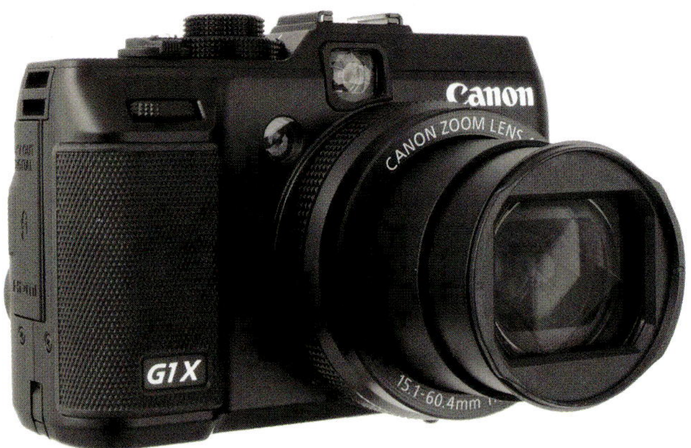

Figure 1.6
The Canon PowerShot G1 X has a large sensor and 14 megapixels of resolution.

Retro Cameras ($100 and up)

This group transcends price and capabilities and revolves more around style. In some cases, these cameras are homages to great classic cameras. In others, the camera harkens back to classic style, but adopts a look that's all its own. These cameras run the gamut from very inexpensive (about $100) to downright pricey (well above $1,000). Some examples of this category include:

- **Minox 60662 DCC.** This tiny rangefinder knock-off has a 5.1MP sensor with a fixed 42mm equivalent lens and 128MB of internal memory. It also takes SDHC memory cards up to 16GB. Compose your images either via the camera's LCD screen or with the included optical viewfinder, a rarity among point-and-shoot cameras these days. (See Figure 1.7.)
- **Rollei Rolleiflex AF5.0 MiniDigi.** I'm old enough to have worked with TLRs (Twin Lens Reflex) cameras. The Rolleiflex A5.0 is a miniaturized digital replica of Rollei's legendary TLRs, right down to viewing the LCD screen on the top of the camera while holding it at waist level and cranking the side crank to set the camera for the next shot.
- **Fujifilm FinePix X100.** The previous two examples are both affordable and decent picture makers, but not necessarily pro caliber machines. The Fujifilm FinePix X100 is a 12MP camera that sports a 35mm equivalent f/2.0 lens that's so retro it's even operated via an aperture ring on the lens. It also sports a hybrid optical/electronic viewfinder. This serious picture-making machine also sports a serious price (hopefully you've figured out that this is the "well above $1,000 camera" alluded to above).

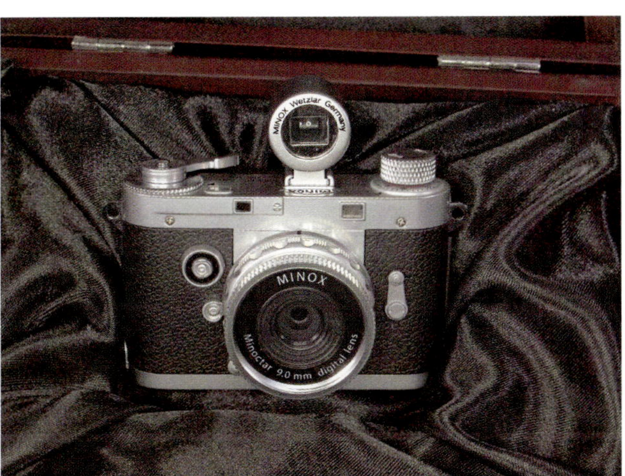

Figure 1.7
While it may look like an antique, the Minox 60662 DCC is a very capable point-and-shoot camera.

- **Olympus OM-D E-M5.** This is another $1,000-plus camera that almost fits in the point-and-shoot category (it can easily be used in point-and-shoot mode), but is definitely a retro model, styled and sized like ancient Olympus OM film cameras. However, its features make it more of a half-scale dSLR, complete with interchangeable Micro Four Thirds lenses and a pentaprism-like "hump" on top that resembles those found in digital SLR cameras.

Chapter 2

Quick Setup Guide

Congratulations! You just bought a new digital point-and-shoot camera. It's time to go out and make some images and get the hang of your new gear. Let's unbox your camera and get it ready for use. This is really pretty simple. Just attach the neck strap, insert the batteries and a memory card, and turn on the camera.

Depending on your camera, you might need to set the date and time. If not, you can probably just start shooting. Of course, it's better if you make some decisions regarding camera settings before you get started.

What's in the Box?

Your new camera comes with various odds and ends to help you begin your photographic journey. The unboxing process should be a careful and thoughtful one to make sure your camera shipped with everything it was supposed to.

Generally, your camera comes with the following:

- **Camera.** As long as you're buying a new or refurbished camera, the basic camera should be packaged on its own, sans battery and camera strap. These things should all be somewhere in the box though.
- **Battery.** If your camera requires a proprietary battery, there should be one in the box. These batteries usually don't have a full charge, so your first step will be to charge the battery with the accompanying battery charger. If your camera relies on AA or AAA batteries, they'll often be included. Take note as to whether you can use any kind of battery, or if you're limited to certain kinds (alkaline versus rechargeable for instance). Save the protective cover that comes with the battery. If you transport a battery outside the camera, it's a good idea to reattach the cover to prevent the electrical contacts from shorting out.

- **Battery charger.** This device is necessary for recharging the battery. In North America, point-and-shoot chargers are usually designed to plug directly into the wall, but in some countries, it includes a plug adapter, or a cable, with the suitable plug for the specific geographic area. This device is often compatible with 100 to 240V 50/60 Hz outlets so when traveling far afield you should not need to use a power converter. Before visiting another country however, be sure to research their power voltage and the plug adapter you'll need to buy; in some countries this can vary from region to region. Adapters of all types are readily available from mail-order companies such as Magellan's. (The www.magellans.com site provides useful specifics for many countries.) Some point-and-shoot cameras have the charger built in to the camera itself, and you can revitalize the battery with a supplied USB cable, simply by plugging one end into the camera, and one end into your computer or a power adapter. (Your cell phone charger may even work just fine, making one less thing for you to carry on vacation.) (See Figure 2.1.)
- **Camera strap.** Your camera comes with a camera strap designed to work with your lightweight point-and-shoot camera. The attachment scheme of your camera may be proprietary and prevent you from using any strap other than the one that comes with the camera. But if you want a fancier, sturdier strap, you may be able to find one from third parties, as described below.
- **Instruction manual.** You'll often find an instruction manual in the box too, either of the printed variety or, more commonly these days, as a PDF file on a CD. The quality of these manuals varies greatly from camera maker to camera maker. Depending on your experience level with digital cameras, you may just start playing with your new camera to learn how it functions or you might resort to reading the manual. Of course if you just read further into this book, I'll try to help you get up to speed as well.

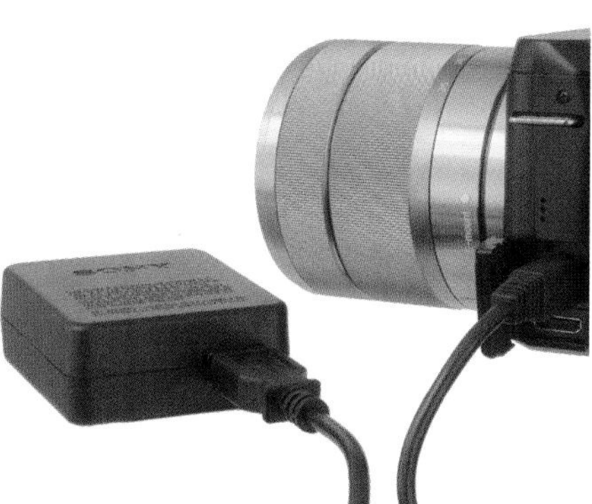

Figure 2.1
A charger of some type will be included with every camera furnished with rechargeable batteries.

- **Software CD.** Your camera will come with a software CD. These CDs generally include an image editing program for manipulating your images and an image cataloging program for helping you organize and track your photos.
- **Cables.** Your camera should come with one or more cables. Generally these include a USB cable to connect your camera to your computer and perhaps an audio/video cable to connect your camera to a television, either standard definition or high definition. While a standard definition cable may be included, most cameras do not include an HDMI cable needed to connect to high-definition televisions.
- **Warranty, safety, and customer support leaflets.** Don't lose these! You can register your camera by mail or (frequently) online. You don't really need to register the camera to keep your warranty in force, but you may need the information in this paperwork (plus the purchase receipt/invoice from your retailer) should you require service support. Since it's not needed for service, why is a warranty card always included? Vendors often have the camera retailer fill out half the card so they can track models as they are sold, and, as a bonus, if you fill out and mail in your half of the card, the vendor now has your name, address, and phone number, which it can use for its own (sometimes nefarious) purposes.

Essential Add-Ons

Your camera comes with much of what you need to get started shooting, but not quite everything. Here's a quick look at a few things you either will or might need:

- **Memory card.** Unless you purchased a camera "bonus" kit of the sort that some retailers bundle together, or bought a used camera that came with a memory card, you're not likely to get one with your camera. Some point-and-shoot cameras do have a limited amount of memory built in for storing pictures, with the capability of copying them from the internal storage to a memory card. That capability is best used for emergencies—when your "real" memory fills up, perhaps. You need a real card with enough capacity to store—at the minimum—all the images you shoot in a single day.

  Of course, less enthusiastic shooters get by with just one card. You know them: they're the folks who have their Thanksgiving and Fourth of July shots on the same memory card. They rarely erase anything, may not even know how to transfer images to their computers, and typically simply take the camera and/or card to the drug store to have prints made as required.

Most of us, however, need at least two: one card for shooting, and a second to use when the first card fills or, in rare emergencies, fails entirely. The typical SD-type card is available in capacities ranging all the way up to 64GB, with sizes for the latest SDXC (Secure Digital Extra Capacity) currently topping out at 256GB. It's unlikely you'll need quite that much storage. A point-and-shoot with 10-14 megapixels of resolution can get by quite nicely with two 8GB or 16GB memory cards; models with higher resolutions justify 16GB or even 32GB cards. Leave the mammoth cards for the advanced photographers, who generally copy and backup their images frequently enough that the "all your eggs in one basket" threat isn't a problem for them.

- **Better camera strap.** While your camera came with a camera strap, there can be many reasons why you might not be satisfied with it. There are many good choices out there, including the UPstrap, which features a non-slip grip, or a Black Rapid strap, which is one of the new sling style straps that positions the camera down by your hip where you can just reach down and slide the camera up the sling to bring it into shooting position.

  For heavier point-and-shoot models, if you want a strap that won't easily slip off your shoulder, I particularly recommend the UPstrap RF Nylon Web model, which is made especially for smaller cameras (but *not* for pocket-sized point-and-shoots). The UPstrap has a patented non-slip pad molded to a 3/8-inch 1,200-pound test nylon webbing, and can be found at www.upstrap.com. (See Figure 2.2.)

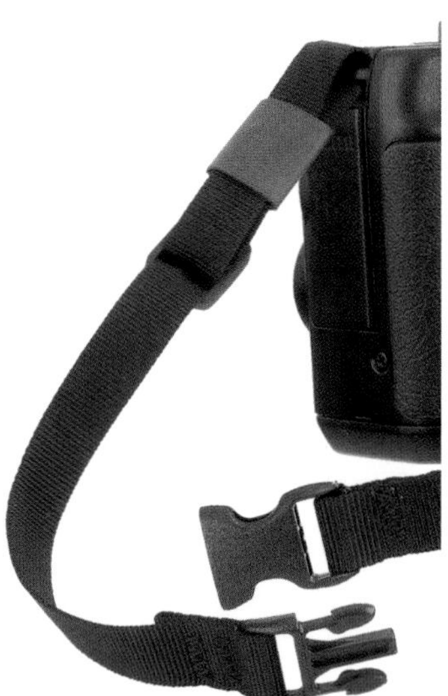

Figure 2.2
You might prefer a non-slip premium strap like the UPstrap.

- **Batteries.** If you use your camera a lot, then an extra battery or two can come in handy, especially since the tiny size of many point-and-shoots limits them to low-capacity batteries that may be good for only a few hundred shots before they need replacement/replenishment. While you can often find plenty of third-party offerings, it's better to stick with batteries made by the camera maker. It's not a great idea to save a few dollars and risk damaging your camera with a battery that may not be up to specs, nor produce the advertised amount of juice. You are more likely to receive a free replacement if the camera manufacturer's battery fails during the warranty period.

Useful Accessories

One of the really attractive things about point-and-shoot cameras is that they don't really need accessories. Chances are, for most shooting situations, a fresh battery and an empty memory card of decent capacity are all you need for a good day of fun and photography. Slip your point-and-shoot in your pocket and go! However, a few accessories can prove useful. For those of us who like to accessorize though, there are options. Some of these will enhance our image-making capabilities; others will appeal to our sense of style.

- **LCD protector.** The LCD on the back of your camera is tough, but one of the joys of using a point-and-shoot camera is being able to handle it like a fun tool, and not a fragile antique. An LCD screen protector may be a good idea, as a dirty and scratched LCD viewer is less pleasant to use, and reduces the resale value of your camera (if you're one of those who enjoys upgrading to the latest and greatest technology every few years).

  There are "skin" type protectors, similar to those applied to the screens of smart phones, as well as thin glass and plastic protectors. If your point-and-shoot has an articulated LCD that reverses against the camera body for protection, you still might want a protector, and should probably consider the film or "skin" variety to avoid adding thickness that will prevent swiveling the LCD to the reverse position. (See Figure 2.3.)
- **Cleaning tools.** It's a good idea to have a bulb blower for blowing dust off your camera body and lens and a microfiber cloth for cleaning your lens. Even though the lens of many point-and-shoot cameras retracts into the body when powered down, your optics can still pick up dust, dirt, and grime. Models with removable lenses may need a puff of air to tidy up their sensor. (See Figure 2.4.)

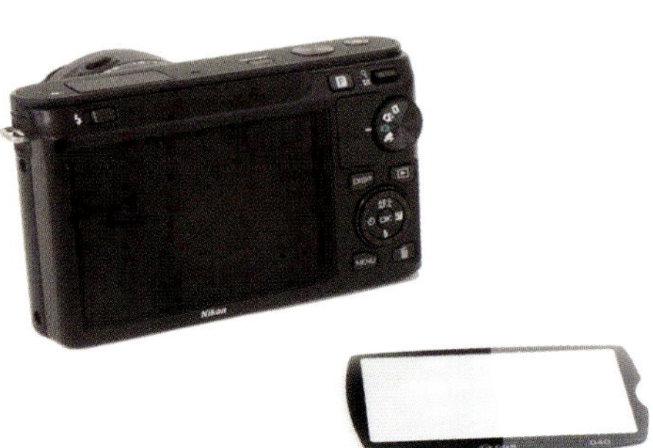

Figure 2.3 A screen protector can be a good investment.

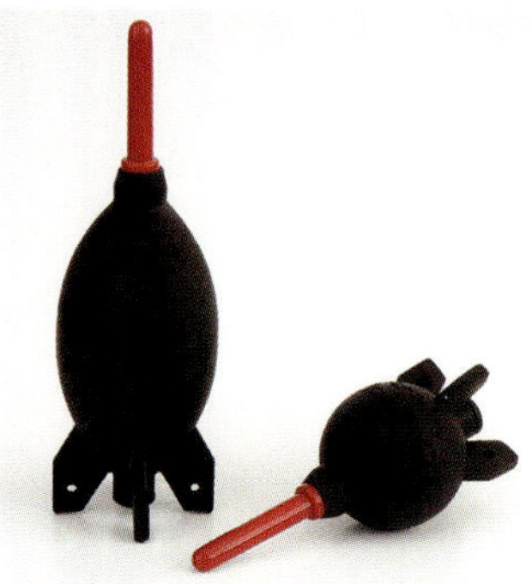

Figure 2.4 A bulb blower can be used to clean your camera body and lens; if your point-and-shoot has interchangeable lenses, you can dust off the sensor, too.

- **Tripod/monopod/clamp.** There are many options for camera support with a point-and-shoot camera. While a dSLR might call for a massive tripod, lighter, flimsier options will serve just fine for a point-and-shoot camera. Options such as the Bogen Super Clamp, Joby Gorillapod, TekTrek Go Pro, or T-Pod all would serve for point-and-shoot support. Another option is the QuikPod, which can be helpful for self-portraits and for extending your reach for unusual camera angles. (See Figure 2.5.)
- **Supplemental lighting.** While most point-and-shoot cameras have built-in flash capabilities, it's often better to try alternative methods of lighting your subject. Even if your point-and-shoot camera doesn't have a hot shoe or other flash connection, there are ways of bringing additional light on your subject. These include "hot" lights (continuous light sources) and "slaved" flash units that can be triggered by the camera's built-in flash. (See Figure 2.6.)
- **Cases/camera bags.** While cases and camera bags are hardly necessary for point-and-shoot cameras, some photographers like the idea of the extra protection such accessories provide, and the ability to carry along some accessories. Form fitting cases provide dust and shock protection while not making the camera much bulkier. If you have to deal with dusty or sandy conditions on a regular basis, and have a larger, non-pocket-sized point-and-shoot, such a case can give your camera a little extra protection.

  If you opt for a small camera bag instead, you can pull your camera out and shoot on a moment's notice. Small camera bags provide space for the camera and accessories plus other odds and ends such as snacks and keys.

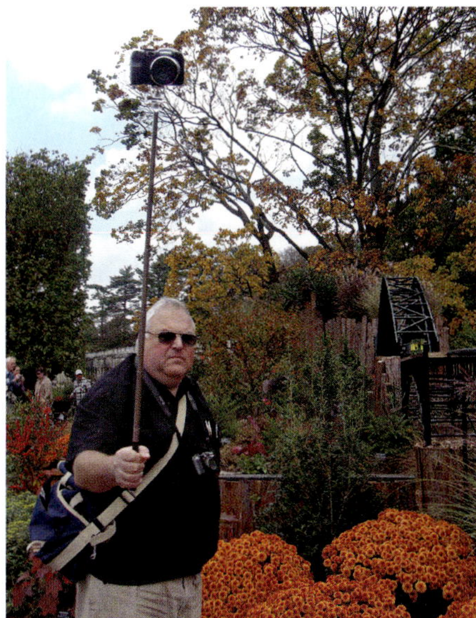

Figure 2.5 Accessories such as the Tek Trek T-Pod or the QuikPod can be helpful additions to a point-and-shoot camera.

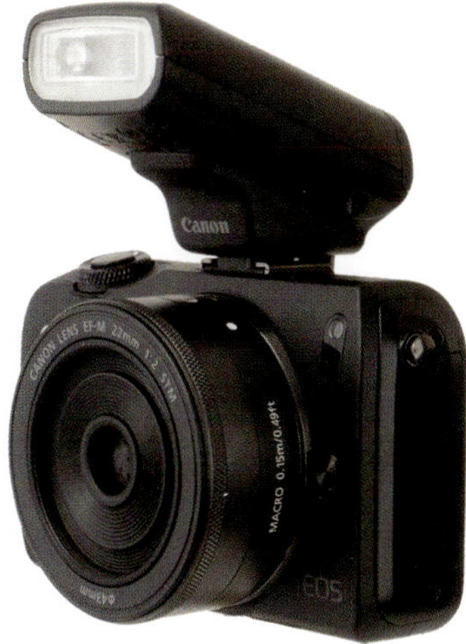

Figure 2.6 An optional add-on flash can give you extra versatility.

Putting Everything Together

There are only a few things you *must* do to get your camera up and running. Attach the camera strap, load the batteries and memory card, and dial in the basic camera settings (time and date, resolution, and other preferences). Generally your point-and-shoot camera will rely on a menu system approach for those settings you don't have to change very often. Normally you reach this system via a Menu button (location varies from camera to camera, but back right side is pretty common). Common menu labels include "Shooting," "Setup," "Custom," and others.

After pressing the Menu button, you usually end up with a choice of two or more submenus (sometimes as many as five). The more sophisticated the camera, the more submenus and the greater the likelihood of tabs running either vertically or horizontally to mark the subfolders. The vast majority of point-and-shoot cameras use arrow keys of some sort for navigating the menu system. Let's look at some initial settings you'll need to set before using your camera. Not all of these will be available with every point-and-shoot, and your camera manual will probably tell you how to make these adjustments quickly and easily:

- **Set the date and time.** Since the camera records shooting information for each image, it's a good idea to take advantage of this capability by making sure the data is accurate. Most cameras can at least record the date and time; many point-and-shoot cameras these days also offer a "home" and a "travel" time option. Often you can also program in your time zone so your camera can adjust to annual time changes.
- **Distance system.** English or Metric system? You may be able to take your pick, if appropriate.
- **LCD brightness.** Choose your preferred LCD brightness. Lower brightness levels save battery power and can be easier to view indoors or in other areas with reduced illumination.
- **Power saving.** Your camera can shut itself off if unused for too long. The delay before turning itself off is set via the Power Saving submenu. Here you can tell the camera how long to wait before shutting down. Most cameras will even let you choose to stay energized if that's what you prefer.
- **Volume.** Controls the volume of video/audio playback.
- **Button options.** Higher-end cameras often offer the ability to change the functions of certain buttons or controls.
- **Silent/Normal.** Turns on/off the various noises the camera makes. These may include start-up sounds, electronically induced "shutter click" noises, countdown timers, and other audio signals.
- **Personal information.** Some cameras let you enter your name or a specific number/letter combination to act as a prefix to the file numbering system. Or, you might be able to affix your name and copyright symbol or other message that will be embedded in each image file as it is stored to your memory card.
- **File numbering.** Do you want the camera to use a continuous numbering system or to reset to one after a certain interval? This submenu lets you make that choice.

With these basics out of the way, you're all set to go out and take a few hundred (or thousand) great pictures. Just set your camera to its Automatic mode (usually marked in green on a dial on the top or back panel of the camera), and go. If you'd like to learn how to use some more advanced controls, you'll find useful information in the next chapter.

Chapter 3

Taking Control

There are hundreds of models of point-and-shoot digital cameras on the market and in the hands of photographers everywhere. Although cataloging every single camera control probably isn't possible or desirable, I can certainly cover enough of the important ones and their variants to make this a useful chapter for you no matter what kind of point-and-shoot camera you own.

Let's face it, when it comes to basic camera controls, certain approaches are virtually universal when it comes to point-and-shoot cameras. I'll go over them first and then try to touch upon unusual options that are less prevalent.

Key Controls

We can start with the basics, namely the power button, shutter release, zoom lever, mode dial, and Menu buttons. These are standard for just about every camera and through them you get your camera up and shooting.

Five controls are all you need for everyday shooting: the power button, shutter release, zoom lever, mode dial, and Menu button.

- **Power button.** The On/Off button design and camera-top placement is standard for point-and-shoot cameras with very few exceptions. One common type is a rotating On/Off switch, as shown at top in Figure 3.1. The switch can be a standalone control (top left), or concentric with the shutter release (top right). Another option is a push button, shown at bottom in Figure 3.1. Slider switches are also used. On/Off controls are usually placed on top of the camera, but sometimes show up on the back by the LCD screen or upper-right back corner of the camera. Fuji's X10 camera and Nikon's V1/J1 models can be activated by turning the camera's zoom ring; others use the Playback button. I have a Minox DCC Leica M3 camera replica, which actually makes the power button a multi-function switch. Pressing and holding it turns the camera on, but after that the power button works as a menu button with the shutter button serving as a "select" button. The camera is then powered off via a menu command rather than with the power button. Note that most cameras have a timer that shuts them off automatically after a given amount of time (you can usually specify the length of the delay), so you may not need to turn your camera off at all.

- **Shutter release.** Once upon a time, pressing the shutter release button did only one thing: take the picture. As cameras became more and more electronic, this button started picking up extra duties and options. At bare minimum, pressing it still takes the photo, but for many cameras, giving it a half press activates the metering and autofocus systems to start the exposure process. With many higher end digital point-and-shoot cameras you can change these settings to ones you might prefer such as autoexposure lock or autofocus lock. You should be able to find the shutter release button quickly in each of the four cameras illustrated in Figure 3.1, even though none of them are explicitly labeled. Aside from the power switch, the shutter release is the easiest control to understand, find, and use.
- **Zoom lever.** This control is generally located somewhere near the front of the camera on its right side. Generally, it's either near the top of the front side of the camera or on the very top of the camera (often concentric with the shutter release button). The zoom lever controls the camera's zooming function in shooting mode. For many cameras, the lever pulls double duty by letting the user examine the image more closely in playback mode, zooming in and out of a magnified image.
- **Mode dial.** This control's basic purpose is to set the camera's exposure mode. However, special modes or features are also chosen using the mode dial. Many cameras use this dial to put the camera in movie, panorama, or special scene modes that handle specific shooting situations.

  This dial is generally located on the top deck of the camera on its right side (as shown at top in Figure 3.2). Some cameras place this dial on the top left or back panel on the right. A few, especially newer models from Canon, have no physical dial at all, using a touch screen instead to adjust shooting mode (Figure 3.2, bottom left). Some Sony models have a "virtual" mode dial that pops on the LCD when you press a button. (Figure 3.2, bottom right.) You can then adjust the shooting mode by spinning a designated (or virtual) dial on the camera.
- **Menu/function button.** Many digital cameras are heavily reliant on their menu commands for controlling the camera, adjusting setup and shooting features, and specifying how images are displayed during playback/review. The menu button is just about always located on the back of the camera

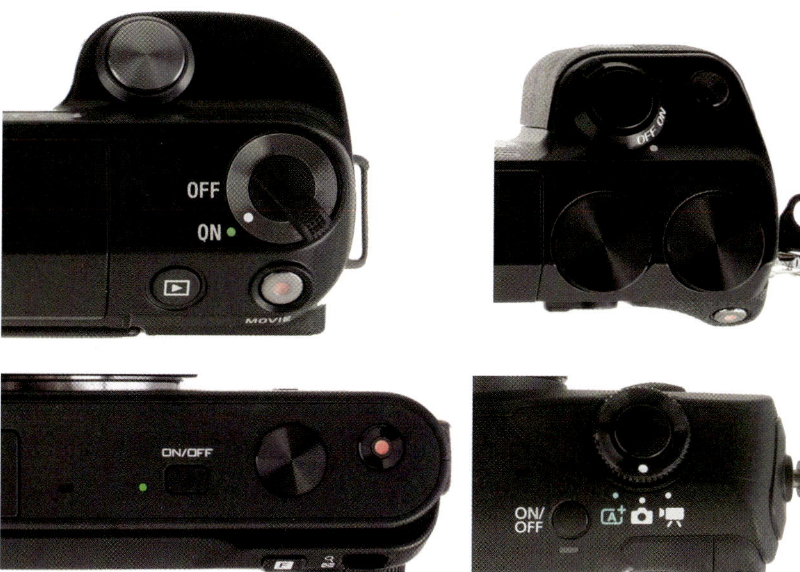

Figure 3.1 Locating the power button and shutter release is easy.

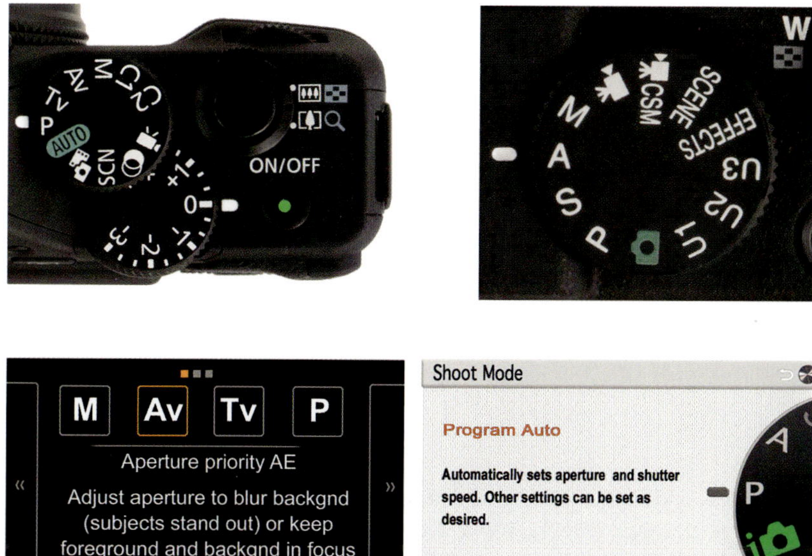

Figure 3.2 Mode dials can be physical (top) or virtual (bottom).

on its right side. (See Figure 3.3.) Placement can be anywhere from the bottom right to the top right of the camera back. Often it is placed inside a control ring, dial, or arrow keypad. Many cameras have a second menu button, often called a Function, Func., or Fn button, which brings up an on-screen display of options overlaid on the current live view image. (See Figure 3.4.) Function button menus are often quicker to access and adjust, and are often used during shooting, whereas the more complex menu button choices are reserved for setting more advanced camera functions.

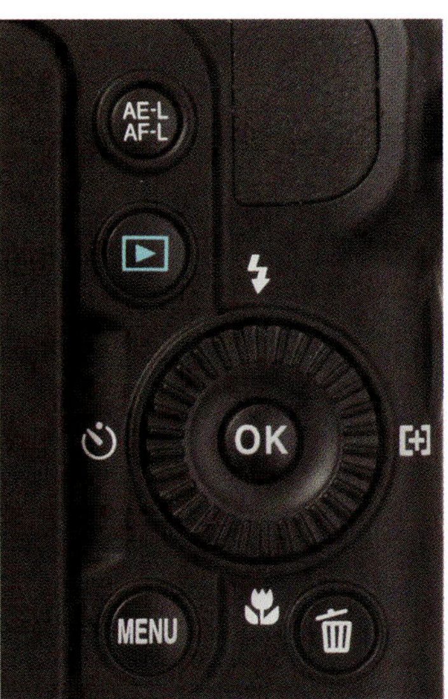

Figure 3.3
The Menu button (lower left) provides access to a variety of setup, shooting, and playback features.

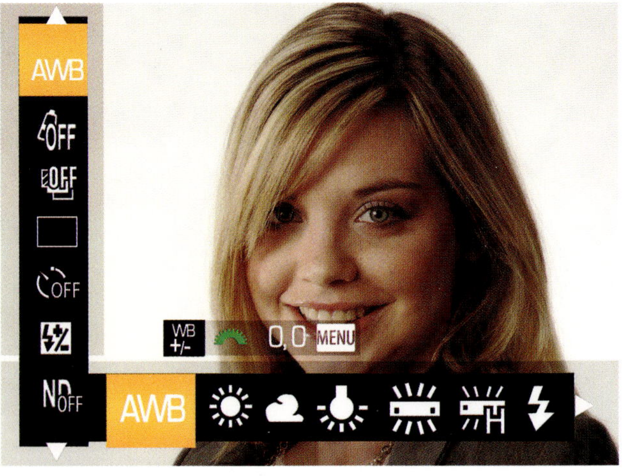

Figure 3.4
Function menus produce a screen of the most common settings for quick adjustments.

Other Important Controls

There are some other standard camera controls that you need to learn about. Some of them, like the Playback button, use an almost universal symbol of a directional triangle pointing right inside a box (see the example upper left in Figure 3.3, earlier). Others, such as control rings and dials and keypads, vary from camera to camera even though they are similar in concept. Most of these will commonly be found on the back of the camera, but once in a while individual buttons may be located on the top or front of the camera.

One of the big questions camera makers wrestle with is whether to make an adjustment button-controlled or menu-controlled. Both approaches have advantages and disadvantages. Buttons are easier and faster for the photographer, but you can only fit so many on the camera. Menu options are almost unlimited in scope, because designers can always add more menu tabs or menu entries. But menus slow the photographer down and can be confusing to navigate. Some cameras rely on deeply nested menu systems (folders within folders within folders) that can drive photographers crazy as they look for a specific control. Most camera makers try to find some kind of workable compromise between physical controls and menu controls, activating the most important controls via physical controls and less often used controls via menus. To increase versatility, many times the buttons can perform more than one action and often the camera will include at least one user-defined button or custom button.

- **Playback button.** Push this button to review your images. This is generally the only function assigned to this button.
- **EVF/LCD button.** On cameras equipped with a back-panel LCD and an eyelevel electronic viewfinder (EVF), this button switches back and forth between the electronic viewfinder and LCD screen for image composition and image playback.
- **Control ring/dial/keypad.** Most point-and-shoot cameras offer some version of this multi-function control. It may be a simple compass style (north, south, east, west) keypad used to navigate through menus, to move focus points from one location to another in the frame in shooting mode, or to scroll around within a zoomed image in playback/review mode. This control might be a combination dial/keypad that can be turned or pushed to control multiple camera functions. While the top/bottom/left/right positions are used for navigation, each may also be assigned a secondary function, as seen in Figure 3.5.
- **Ok/Set/Enter button.** This button is used to confirm your selections. Sometimes it's a function of the Menu button, or located in the center of the keypad, or assigned to a dedicated button.

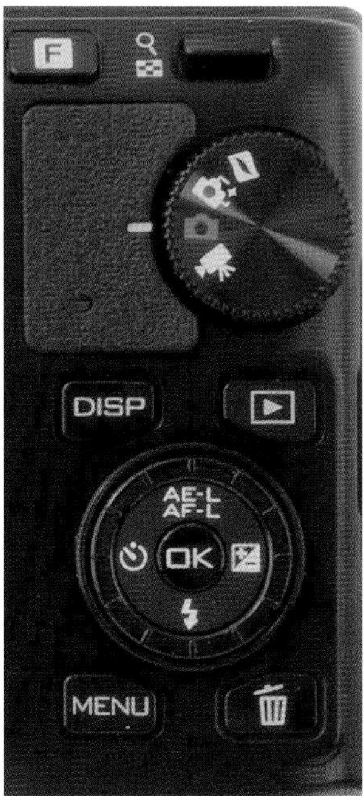

Figure 3.5
Point-and-shoot cameras often designate multiple uses for the various buttons, levers, and dials found on the camera.

- **Display/Info button.** Your camera's display is capable of showing quite a bit of information. Depending on your camera, it's usually either called the "Display" or "Info" button. Each time you press it, the camera display changes revealing more or less information. Some cameras let you configure these views to your preferences. In playback mode the display can provide you with information about the image such as exposure settings, histograms, and other data.
- **Exposure compensation button (+/-).** Some cameras put this button on the top deck near the shutter release or power button; some put it on the back of the camera. Press it and you'll be asked to choose the amount of exposure compensation you need. "Plus" settings provide greater exposure (brighter photos), while "minus" settings reduce exposure (darker photos).
- **Trash button.** Often, this delete button is a separate control with a trash can icon printed on it or next to it.
- **Flash pop-up button.** While your camera may have a flash control button, this is not the button that extends its pop-up flash if it has one (most point-and-shoot cameras have a built-in flash, but not all of them have a flash that pops up). Usually the flash activation button is located somewhere near the flash.

- **None of the above.** Some buttons are less common. It's not unusual for a higher-end point-and-shoot camera to include an optical viewfinder. These usually include a diopter adjustment control so you can tweak the viewfinder for your eyesight. Others have a special button for protecting images or marking photos for DPOF (Digital Print Order Format) printouts. Buttons may also control the continuous shooting options, face recognition, or anti-shake control.

Ports and Connections

On the left or right side of your point-and-shoot camera, you'll find a flip-open door that protects/conceals anywhere from two to five sockets, or ports, that can be used to connect your camera to the outside world. Figure 3.6 shows the three most common connectors; your model may have more. Here's what they are for:

- **Microphone jack**. Although the least expensive point-and-shoot will have the capability of shooting good-quality video, their built-in monaural or stereo microphones may not produce the best sound quality. As you move up to more advanced models, sockets are built in to plug in an inexpensive (or pricier) microphone. An external mic improves sound quality and allows you to place the microphone away from the camera and closer to your sound source.

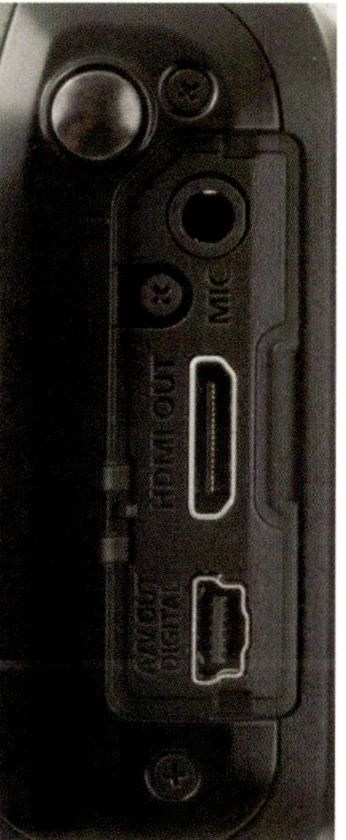

Figure 3.6
Common connectors include a microphone jack (top), HDMI port (middle), and USB/AV connector (bottom).

- **HDMI port.** Your camera's HDMI port makes it possible to connect your camera to your HDTV and view high-quality images and video on your television.
- **Mini-USB connection.** While it's most likely your camera will have a mini-USB connection, it is possible it will have a different version of this connection. The primary reason for this port is so you can connect your camera to your computer, either for firmware updates or to transfer images.
- **A/V Out.** Your camera may have a lower-quality audio/video output connection for use when HDMI is not available or if you don't have an HDMI cable for your camera. (Many camera makers provide an A/V cable for your camera but not an HDMI cable.) Many newer point-and-shoot models combine this port with the USB socket to save space.
- **Remote release port.** Some more advanced point-and-shoot cameras can be used with an optional wired remote control that plugs into the corresponding port.
- **Hot shoe.** The more advanced the point-and-shoot camera, the more likely it is to have a portable flash hot shoe installed on top of the camera. This is a useful and important enough feature to justify choosing a specific camera because it has a hot/accessory shoe over a camera that doesn't. While using a decent shoe mount flash with your point-and-shoot can improve your images (particularly if you get one that can swivel and tilt), the hot shoe can also be used to trigger remote flash units via a number of accessories the market offers, and provides a mounting point for other optional accessories, such as external microphones and GPS devices that can embed location information in your image files. (See Figure 3.7.)

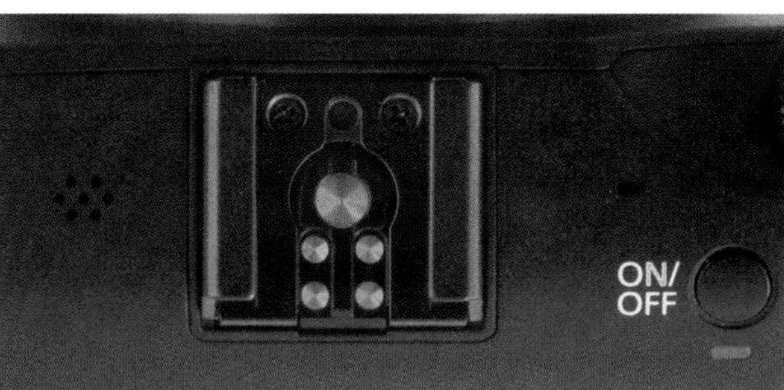

Figure 3.7
A hot shoe makes your camera more versatile since it makes it possible for you to use portable flash units or other accessories.

Understanding Menus

A digital camera's menu system is often a source of frustration and bewilderment to many new camera owners. Designers usually try to group menu choices by purpose. Some common examples include the Playback menu, Shooting menu, and Setup menu.

Your camera probably uses terms such as "folders," "tabs," or "menus." You press the Menu button to activate the menu screen and then use the command dial or arrow pad to navigate to the appropriate tab or folder. Once you've entered a menu screen, you continue with the directional controls to navigate to the desired submenu. Once the submenu is chosen, you can then adjust the particular setting. Each of these menu tabs/folders provides some important options for you to consider.

Shooting Menu

This typical menu (see Figure 3.8) controls options that can directly affect the picture-making process (compared to the Setup menu which controls things like date and time, numbering, and other non image-making settings). Chances are good you won't need to change Setup menu items during the course of a shoot, but you'll probably have to turn to the Shooting menu at least occasionally. While your Shooting menu options will vary from camera to camera, here are some typical settings found in many cameras:

- **Resolution.** This is the pixel density of the image you're creating. Your camera should offer you the ability to select from several different resolution settings, often labeled Large, Medium, and Small. Your manual will tell you what resolution each of these choices provides. Most of the time resolution is one of those settings you don't change during a shoot. It's also not unusual for a camera to change the resolution setting to a lower value when you go to an extremely high ISO setting or take advantage of a high dynamic range (extended tonal range) feature the camera offers. (What the camera is doing is combining or pooling information from several pixels to provide a better quality/lower noise image, at the cost of some resolution.)
- **Image size.** While resolution controls pixel density, the image size setting controls the height and width dimensions of the image. This also affects the image proportions, as many cameras will let you switch from various format ratios. You might be able to select from 4:3, 3:2, 16:9 (the same proportions as HDTV), panorama (wide screen), or 1:1 (square).

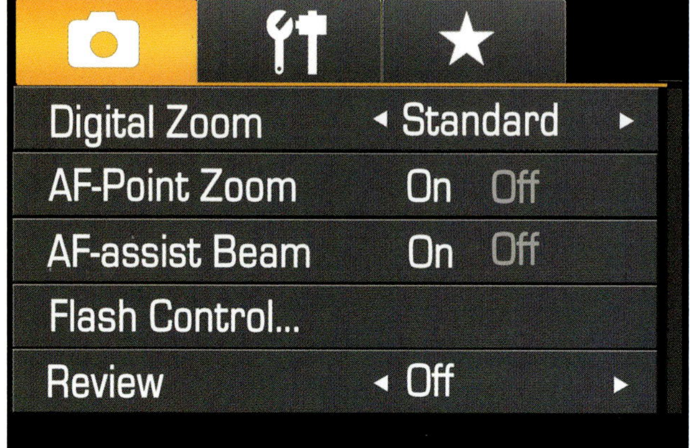

Figure 3.8
Your camera's Shooting menu contains many of the controls you need to optimize your images.

- **Image quality.** This setting refers to the amount of "squeezing" done to reduce the size of the image and cut down on the amount of storage space required on your memory card. Some quality is lost at higher compression settings, but you'll be able to fit more images on the card. Typical settings are named Super Fine, Fine, Normal, and Basic.
- **ISO.** If you don't have an ISO button to adjust the sensitivity of your sensor, then you'll find the ISO control here. You can either judge what ISO sensitivity you'll need based on the anticipated shooting conditions or you can set your camera to its Auto-ISO setting, which automatically chooses what it considers to be the best ISO choice for the shooting conditions. If you do need to change ISO during a shoot, it's faster and easier to do it if your camera has a button for changing ISO rather than relying on the menu system. Many point-and-shoots have both methods.
- **Self-timer.** This is another control—one of the so-called "drive" modes—that is often found in different places on point-and-shoot cameras. If yours doesn't have a drive mode button control, then it will be in the Shooting menu.
- **Sharpness.** Some cameras offer this setting. You choose the amount of in-camera image sharpening that is applied to the file (virtually all digital cameras perform a certain amount of in-camera image sharpening; some provide more user control than others).
- **White balance.** While some cameras do offer a physical white balance control to adjust the camera for the color bias of your light source (for example, daylight, shade, flash, incandescent, fluorescent), most digital point-and-shoot cameras control this via the menu system, most often in the Shooting menu.

- **Flash controls.** There are several different flash controls your camera may offer, including whether to turn the built-in flash on (if it has one) and what flash settings you prefer (red-eye reduction, automatic flash, forced/fill flash, etc.). Another control is flash exposure compensation, namely adjusting flash output to produce more or less light when the flash is triggered.
- **Autofocus controls.** Many point-and-shoot cameras offer several different options for autofocus. Usually the basic choices are continuous autofocus (where the lens continues to follow a moving subject) versus single shot (when the shutter button is pressed halfway, the camera achieves focus and doesn't shift from that focus point unless the shutter button is half pressed again).

  At a bare minimum, a good point-and-shoot camera should let you choose from among manual focus, single shot autofocus (lock focus when you press the shutter release halfway), and continuous autofocus (refocus as you frame the image, beginning either when you press the shutter release halfway or, with some cameras, continually after you bring the camera up to your eye). Higher-end cameras may offer even more choices.
- **AF assist.** Many cameras have an optional AF assist feature, a beam of light that helps the camera "see" subjects while attempting to focus on them automatically. Of course, the AF assist beam may confuse or distract your subject. This can be particularly frustrating when photographing animals since the light can be enough to startle or scare them away. Heavy use of the AF assist beam can also drain the battery faster.
- **Image stabilization.** This control turns your camera's "anti-shake" or image stabilization feature on or off, or chooses from one of several I.S. settings. Most cameras offer at least on, off, and a panning setting to adjust for intentional side-to-side motion. Some will instead offer a vertical and a horizontal I.S. option.
- **Custom.** Lets you save favorite combinations of settings. Sometimes called "Favorites," "User Settings," or "My Settings."

Playback Menu

The Playback menu (see Figure 3.9) may not actually appear until you're reviewing images in Playback mode. As you'd expect, this menu provides options that have to do with reviewing and managing images. Many cameras include a range of image-editing tools so you can skip the need for a separate computer. Thanks to printer technology that makes it possible to print directly from a digital camera or memory card, you can take care of image processing in-camera and then designate which images are to be printed and even how

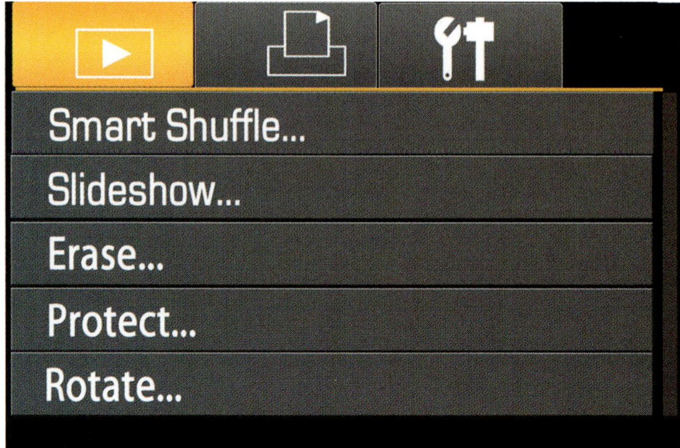

Figure 3.9
Your camera's Playback menu can offer image editing and printing options.

many prints of each image should be made. Some cameras also let you designate images for upload to photo gallery websites or social networking sites. Playback menu options can vary wildly from camera to camera. Although there's not room to cover every possible option here, I'll try to list a good number of them.

- **Slideshow.** Most point-and-shoot digital cameras can be connected to a television to display images. Recognizing this, camera makers have included the ability to present a slideshow of images (often with audio) on your external display or the camera's LCD monitor.
- **Delete/Erase.** While your camera probably has a "trash" button for deleting images, it will usually also offer a menu-based image erasure option too. Often you'll be able to review and designate images for deletion in batches rather than one at a time, making this option better for housekeeping during a break or at the end of a shoot.
- **Protect.** You can protect specific images with this control. Just keep in mind that protecting an image doesn't stop it from being deleted if you format your memory card. It only protects the image if you're erasing the card, not formatting it.
- **Rotate.** If you've turned auto rotate off, you can rotate an image manually via this tool.
- **Red-eye correction.** Fix red eye via this submenu.
- **Trimming/Resizing.** Many cameras let you trim an image to various print sizes or resize the image from a file size standpoint.
- **Reset.** Returns all camera settings to the factory default settings.

- **Blink detection.** The better the camera, the more likely it is to have this feature. When turned on, it warns you that a subject in your photograph may have blinked.
- **Red-eye removal.** Some point-and-shoot cameras offer an automatic red-eye removal function. Be careful about relying on this one though. If your subject is wearing reddish clothing that is similar in color to typical red eye, the camera may also "correct" this red.
- **Select image/range.** You can pick one image or a range of images via this control. Once selected, you can usually designate them for printing or deletion.
- **Print settings.** You can mark your images for printing with this setting. Generally you can select images and mark how many prints you want from each.
- **Mark for upload.** Your camera may let you mark images/videos for upload to social networking or video sites.
- **Voice memo.** This feature lets you add a voice memo to an image. This can be useful in several ways, including annotating an image with location or background information or for getting your subject to leave a message or thought to go with the photo.

Setup Menu

This menu (see Figure 3.10) controls more fundamental options such as date and time, numbering, and other non image-making settings. Chances are good you won't need to change Setup menu items during the course of a shoot,

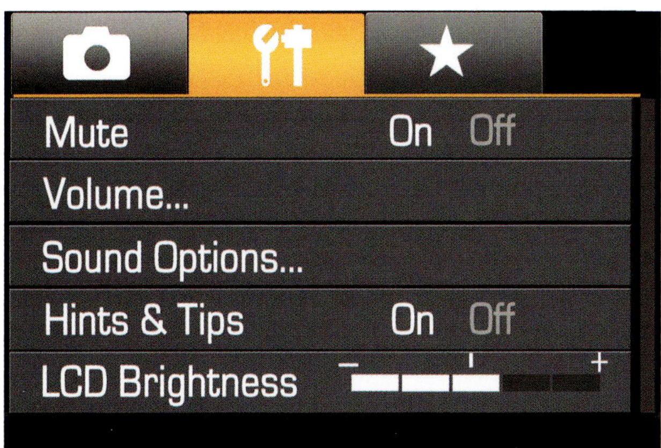

Figure 3.10
The Setup menu is used to maintain many non photographic settings.

whereas you'll probably have to turn to the Shooting menu at least once or twice (or much more often). Your Setup menu options will vary from camera to camera, but here are some typical settings found in many cameras:

- **Date and time.** One of the great things about digital cameras is their ability to record EXIF (Exchangeable Image File Format), which records all sorts of image information every time you make a photo. This includes embedding the date and time the image was created in the file. Modern cameras can also be set to be aware of the time zone you're in and whether daylight savings time is in effect.
- **Format/card setup.** This option lets you turn a full memory card into an empty one. You're always better off handling this task with your camera rather than your computer. The issue of "formatting" versus "erasing the card" (your usual two options) requires more thought. Formatting the card wipes it completely (including any protected images). Erasing all images will erase everything except images you've protected. You should try to format the card every once in a while no matter what, but otherwise merely erasing the card is fine.
- **File numbering.** If your camera offers this option, you'll be able to choose between continuous numbering, 100 number increments, or by adding a date code to the file number.
- **Power saving.** You can determine how long your camera remains on before going into sleep mode or shutting down to save battery power.
- **Video system.** Select NTSC video, which is used in the United States and Canada, or PAL, which is used in Europe and other regions of the world. Your camera may also let you choose between HD quality video and a lower quality setting.
- **Language.** Just about every point-and-shoot digital camera offers a variety of language options so you can set it to your desired language.
- **Reset.** Returns all camera settings to the factory default settings.
- **Blink detection.** When turned on, it warns you that your subject may have blinked.
- **Red-eye removal.** Some point-and-shoot cameras offer an automatic red-eye removal function. Be careful about relying on this one though. If your subject is wearing reddish clothing that is similar in color to typical red eye, the camera may also "correct" this red.
- **Auto rotate.** Many cameras will auto rotate vertical images when you view them on the LCD screen. Although it seems like a nice feature, the result is a smaller review image than if you have the camera leave vertical images horizontally oriented.

- **Image display.** How long does the LCD screen display the image you just created? Well, you get to make this decision with most digital cameras these days.
- **Volume.** Many point-and-shoot digital cameras have built-in speakers for playing back movie clip audio. Some can add audio to an image slideshow when you're reviewing your images on camera or on a big-screen TV.
- **Silent mode.** Point-and-shoot digital cameras don't actually have a mirror return or mechanical shutter, so the typical sound of a camera making a photo doesn't actually occur. Instead, this is a sound effect produced by the camera to provide a familiar, reassuring sound to confirm everything worked as it was supposed to. Some cameras let you turn this sound effect off, so you can work more discreetly.

Using Display Information

Point-and-shoot camera displays are versatile sources of information that can provide either a lot or a little information depending on what you prefer. Depending on whether you prefer to compose images via the camera's viewfinder (some cameras offer an optical viewfinder, others use an electronic display) or its LCD screen, your display information can tell you what modes your camera is using, exposure information, and more.

Most cameras can display a variety of information whether you're using the LCD for shooting or reviewing images. This information is often very useful because it helps you make adjustments when they can do you the most good, while you're still shooting.

Sometimes the amount of information shown can be overwhelming, as you can see in Figure 3.11. Don't panic! No point-and-shoot camera shows that much information all at one time; the figure illustrates every possible data indicator available with that particular camera. In real-life conditions, only a half-dozen or fewer indicators will be shown, and, with most cameras, you can hide or reduce the amount of information by pressing a button to cycle through the optional displays. This button may be labeled Info or Disp. The information shown varies, depending on whether you are shooting images or reviewing pictures you've taken in playback mode. The next sections will familiarize you with both.

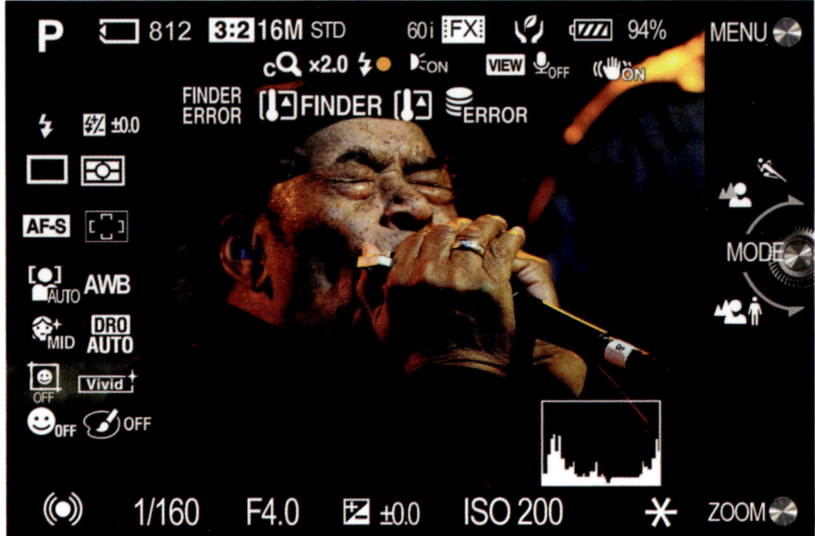

Figure 3.11 Fortunately, most point-and-shoot cameras will show only a small number of information indicators at one time; this figure shows every possible option for one camera.

Exposure Information While Shooting

Your shooting display can provide basic information so you can keep your screen as distraction free as possible, or, it can provide you as much information as possible so you can actively manage settings and make decisions based on camera feedback. Let's look at what your display can tell you, including a lot of what was displayed in Figure 3.11, earlier:

- **Shutter speed.** Shows the current shutter speed setting. Depending on your camera, this display may blink on and off to warn you the shutter speed is too slow to prevent blur from camera shake. Faster shutter speeds (such as 1/125th to 1/1,000th second) freeze action; slower speeds (from 1/60th to 1 second or slower) can cause blur from both camera and subject movement. Image stabilization (described next) or a tripod can counter camera movement. Subject movement can only be frozen by using a higher shutter speed (or flash, which has a brief burst that acts like a higher shutter speed).
- **Image stabilization.** This feature helps keep your camera steady and prevents blur from camera shake. Your LCD should display whether your anti-shake feature is active.
- **Lens opening ("f/stop" or aperture).** Shows the current f/stop setting, or size of the lens opening.

- **Face recognition.** If your camera has the ability to locate faces, your LCD screen will often show this option is active, and can indicate which face or faces is being interpreted.
- **Exposure compensation.** Exposure compensation takes the exposure calculated by the camera's metering system, and then adds or subtracts from that to make the picture lighter or darker. Use it to customize the tonal values of your image and, in effect, "override" the exposure set by the camera. Usually indicated by a +/- icon, this setting shows the amount (if any) of exposure compensation the camera is set to provide.
- **Picture/Scene mode.** Many cameras offer special picture or scene modes designed to cope with specific shooting situations (such as Sports, Portraits, Night Scenes) or offer color/exposure handling options such as replicating color transparency or black-and-white film. This display element will let you know if you're using any of these features. Since some cameras offer multiple options (picture mode, scene mode, filters, etc.), it's possible to have multiple icons displayed for such settings.
- **Battery level.** How much juice does your battery have left? Your display should provide this information.
- **Flash setting.** The display generally shows flash status, such as disabled/ready/charging.
- **AF mode.** Lets you know what autofocus mode you've set.
- **Continuous shooting mode.** Shows whether you're in continuous shooting "burst" mode, single-shot mode, or self-timer mode.
- **ISO.** Displays what sensitivity level the sensor is set for.
- **Light metering pattern.** Many point-and-shoot cameras offer a choice of metering patterns, such as Evaluative, Center-weighted, or Spot. Your display will probably show the pattern your camera is using.

Exposure Information During Playback

When it comes time to review your images, the playback screen display can provide lots of useful information. This information can help you make decisions on subsequent camera settings or alert you to problems with your current choices.

Depending on your camera, you may be able to change information or the number of screens displayed during playback to meet your own shooting style. If so, these changes will be made via the camera's menu system. These displays can vary from camera to camera and from display screen to display screen on the same camera. Here's what you can expect your camera to provide. You'll need to explore your camera's manual or various third-party guidebooks (I may have written one for your camera) to learn how to use these tools:

- **Grayscale or Color (Red/Green/Blue) histogram.** This shows the distribution of pixels throughout the image and is a more precise indicator of contrast and exposure problems than viewing the image on your camera's LCD display.
- **Metering pattern used.** The screen usually displays an icon to indicate which metering pattern the camera used in making the image.
- **Shot sequence on memory card.** Displays the image's place in the sequence of images on the memory card (for example: 39/112 would mean the file is the 39th image out of 112 photos currently stored on the memory card).
- **Exposure mode.** Shows the exposure mode used in making the image.
- **Exposure information.** Shows the shutter speed, f/stop, and ISO settings used in making the image.
- **Exposure compensation.** Shows the amount (if any) of exposure compensation used in making the image.
- **White balance.** Shows the white balance setting used in making the image.
- **File size.** Shows the compressed file size of the image. (Useful for seeing how much space the file takes up on the memory card).
- **Resolution.** Shows the image resolution and size.
- **Image size/compression.** Shows the image quality and compression settings used in making the image. This information is usually displayed with a symbol/letter combination such as a quarter circle and an L to indicate an image shot under highest quality JPEG compression and Large file size.
- **Date and time.** Shows the date and time the image was made.
- **Zoom in/out.** Lets you zoom in and out to examine parts of the image more closely.

Basic Camera Techniques

If you want to get the most out of your camera, then mastering pro camera techniques will help you greatly. Although the term "point-and-shoot" implies you don't have to do much to take pictures, there are still things you can do to improve your results. "Point-and-shoot" cameras are certainly easier to use than dSLRs and other pro-oriented cameras, but that doesn't mean technique has become unnecessary. In some ways holding and operating your camera properly may be even more important with these little gems.

Holding the Camera

Learning how to hold a camera properly can help make its controls more accessible to you and can also improve how steady you can hold the camera. While image stabilization technology makes blur from camera shake less likely, it doesn't eliminate it completely. Hand-holding the camera properly along with image stabilization means you can keep shooting even when conditions are getting darker and darker.

Unfortunately, holding a camera properly has become a lot more complicated these days thanks to the many different camera designs. Camera technique depends on the shape of your camera and how you're using it.

Hand-Holding While Composing the Image with the LCD Screen

This technique calls for holding the camera at arm's length or at least some distance from your face. It's not the most effective method because it's more likely to induce vibration and blur from camera shake. One way of improving your hand-holding technique is to create a platform to rest the camera on instead of using both hands to hold the sides of the camera, then pressing your elbows tightly against your body. Also, extend one leg in front of the other and turn your rear foot perpendicularly to the direction the camera is pointed.

Hand-Holding While Composing the Image via the Camera's Viewfinder

It's easier to make good photos by holding the camera against your face (providing another point of support) so the viewfinder method is a worthwhile option when you're shooting under low light conditions. Just like in the previous guideline, you want to create a platform to rest the camera on instead of using both hands to hold the sides of the camera, then press your elbows tightly against your body. Also, extend one leg in front of the other and turn your rear foot perpendicularly to the direction the camera is pointed. Also, if your camera has a finger grip, then make sure to take advantage of it. (See Figure 3.12.)

Pressing the Shutter

Tripping the shutter is another element of picture making that can reduce the quality of the final image. Use too much pressure or a rapid jerky motion, and you're probably going to have problems with image sharpness. Your goal when tripping the shutter is to gently squeeze the shutter release rather than pressing it.

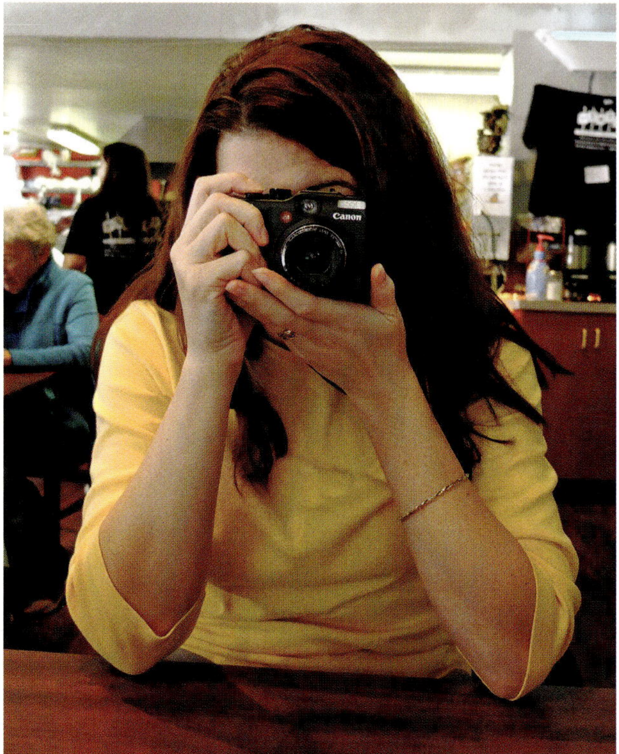

Figure 3.12
When composing your image via the camera's viewfinder, make sure you place one hand under the camera body and press your elbow against your body to hold the camera steady.

Vertical Versus Horizontal Composition

All too often, photographic composition is determined more by the shape of the camera than the eye of the photographer. Since just about every point-and-shoot camera is horizontally oriented, most of the time images from these cameras tend to be horizontally composed. Turning the camera vertically can actually improve your photographic composition by using space more effectively and using the orientation to match that of your subject.

You can even vary your orientation when shooting the same subject, as shown in Figures 3.13 and 3.14. Horizontal compositions emphasize width and expansiveness, especially in the panorama shown in Figure 3.13. (Many point-and-shoot cameras offer a panorama mode that can combine two or more shots into one wide-screen image.) Vertical compositions underscore height. Even though Figure 3.14 shows the same Prague castle pictured in the previous image, the vertical composition emphasizes the structure's commanding position high above the city proper.

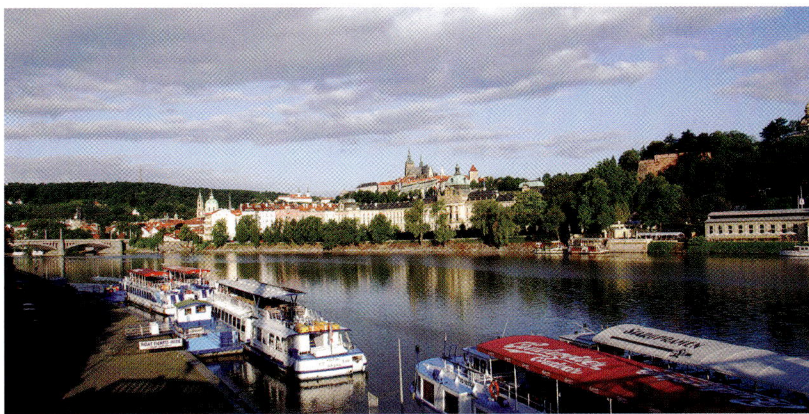

Figure 3.13 Horizontal compositions are best for broad expanses of scenery.

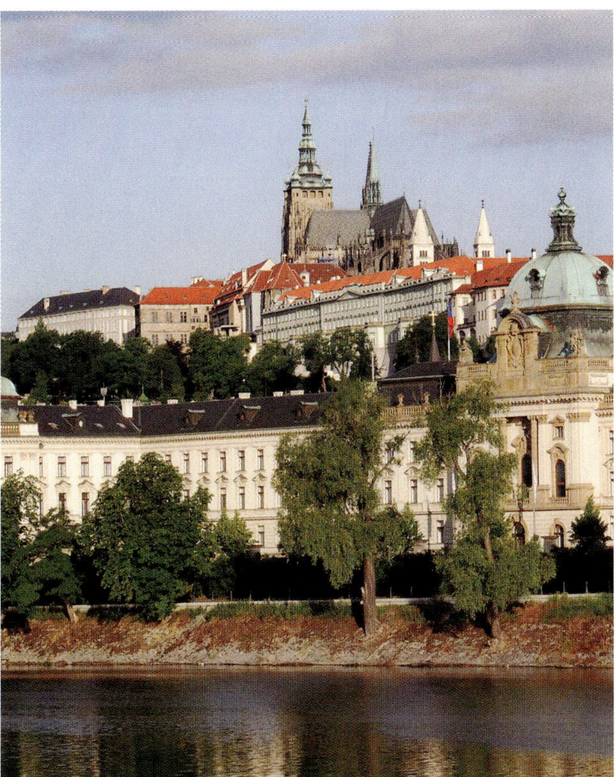

Figure 3.14 Vertical compositions emphasize height.

Chapter 4

Exploring Key Features

In this chapter, we'll look at your camera's most commonly used features for controlling exposure, autofocus, zooming, drive modes, and flash exposures.

Controlling Exposure

Exposure determines whether your point-and-shoot camera's images appear to be too dark, too light, or just right. Even the simplest point-and-shoot camera offers a variety of tools for controlling and adjusting exposure. The place to start is with the basic automated "scene" modes, which are programmed to provide an array of settings tailored for specific types of subjects or scenes. By choosing a scene mode, you are telling your camera that you want to shoot a portrait, a landscape, a sports action shot, or shoot on the beach or in snow. Or perhaps you're specifying that your subject will be a pet, a candlelit dinner, or a festive party. The point-and-shoot camera's built-in smarts understand all these types of situations, and it is ready with settings that will help you get the best picture possible without requiring any further input from you.

Using Scene Modes

While the names of various scene modes, or the camera's route to accessing them may differ, the basic idea behind scene modes is similar from camera to camera. The purpose of scene modes is to help the photographer best handle certain common shooting situations more capably than via one of the semi-automatic/manual modes (Program, Aperture-priority, Shutter-priority, or Manual modes, discussed later). With scene modes, all you have to do is identify the type of shooting scenario you're dealing with and then set your camera to the proper scene mode. Few cameras will have all of these, but most will have at least a few of them. In Chapter 3, I explained how to access scene modes and other exposure modes using the mode dial.

- **Portrait.** Use this mode when you're taking a portrait of a human subject standing relatively close to the camera. The camera will select a shutter speed and aperture that will emphasize the subject, maximize sharpness, and produce flattering skin tones.
- **Landscape.** Select this mode when you want extra sharpness and rich colors of distant scenes. The built-in flash and AF-assist illuminator are often disabled.
- **Child.** Use this mode to accentuate the vivid colors often found in children's clothing, and to render skin tones with a soft, natural-looking texture. This scene mode frequently uses faster shutter speeds to freeze the movements of active children.
- **Sports.** Use this mode to stop fast-moving subjects, and minimize motion blur. The camera selects a fast shutter speed to stop this action, and focuses continuously, usually using the center focus point, for as long as you have the shutter release button pressed halfway. The built-in electronic flash and focus assist illuminator lamp are often disabled.
- **Close-up/Macro.** This mode is helpful when you are shooting close-up pictures of a subject from about one foot away or less, such as flowers, bugs, and small items. The camera focuses on the closest subject in the center of the frame, but you can adjust focus on a different point if desired. Use a tripod in this mode, as small apertures may be selected to increase the depth-of-field (range of sharpness), causing exposures long enough to cause blurring from camera movement. The built-in flash may pop up or flash if needed.
- **Night portrait.** Choose this mode when you want to illuminate a subject in the foreground with flash (it will probably pop up automatically, if needed), but still allow the background to be exposed properly by the available light. The camera usually focuses on the closest main subject. Be prepared to use a tripod or image stabilization to reduce the effects of camera shake with the long shutter speeds that frequently result.
- **Fireworks.** When you set your camera to Fireworks mode, its programming will choose a slow shutter speed and color settings to capture and possibly enhance the colors of the fireworks display. Try to use a tripod or place your camera on a wall or car roof to keep it as steady as possible.
- **Sunrise/Sunset/Dusk/Dawn.** This mode chooses settings designed to capture the rich, saturated colors of sunrise and sunset. Some cameras have individual settings for each of these times of day, or may combine them all into a single scene mode.
- **Snow.** In very bright surroundings, your camera's light meter may be fooled into underexposing images. On snowy days, the camera reads all

that bright white and interprets it, incorrectly, as a shade of gray. Setting your camera to Snow mode lets it know it needs to compensate for that condition, giving you more accurately exposed photos.

- **Beach.** This is another scenario where your camera's light meter is likely to be fooled due to brighter conditions than it's been programmed to expect. Some cameras combine Snow/Beach into a single scene mode setting.
- **Underwater.** Please don't dunk your camera unless it's specifically labeled as an "underwater" model! This setting means only that the camera will compensate for typical underwater lighting conditions (rapid light falloff and loss of certain color wavelengths). Camera makers include this scene mode on point-and-shoot cameras because there are often inexpensive underwater housings available. (In fact it can be easier and cheaper to get into underwater photography with a good point-and-shoot camera and underwater housing than it is with a more advanced camera, such as a digital SLR.) Figure 4.1 shows an image created with a Canon PowerShot and an inexpensive underwater housing.

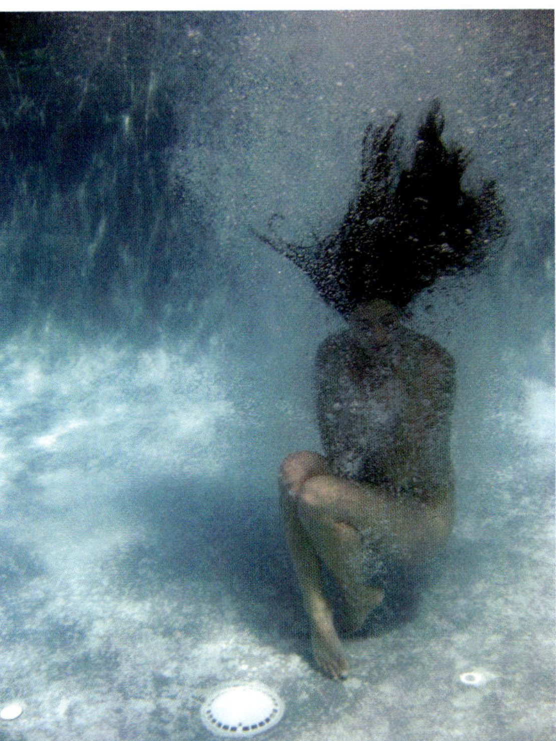

Figure 4.1
Underwater photography produces some interesting effects.

- **Party.** This setting is for parties when the lights are low. It helps record background lighting. It also takes control of ISO sensitivity in order to choose the best setting for the scene. It may boost the value to allow the camera to capture images in lower light, if required.
- **Text.** Use this mode, which emphasizes contrasty, black-and-white images, when you need to turn your camera into a document scanner. Make sure you hold the camera parallel to the surface you're copying. Any tilting will result in parts of the image being out of focus.
- **Natural light.** Use this mode for shooting available light images in low light conditions. Some cameras offer a second version (Natural Light plus Flash). In this mode the camera shoots two photos, one with flash and one without.
- **Enhanced skin.** This is a nice option for creating pleasing portraits. Its main contribution is to smooth the subject's skin (much like what's done in fashion magazines to make the models look perfect). (See Figure 4.2.)

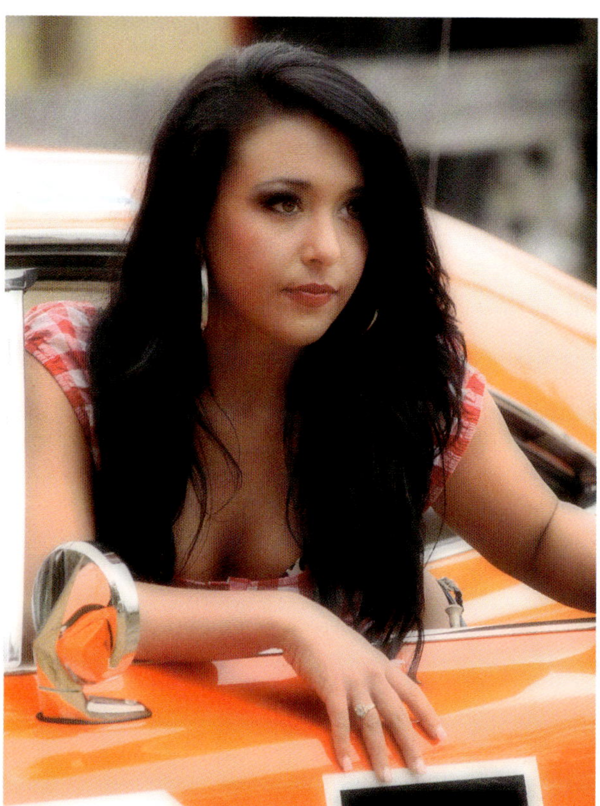

Figure 4.2
Enhanced skin or "skin smoothing" is a popular function for improving your subject's appearance.

- **Low light.** This is another option for times when available light is lacking. In this setting, the camera will take over setting the ISO.
- **Aquarium.** While shooting fish in a barrel may be a piece of cake, photographing fish in an aquarium is a different story. There are several problems you and your camera must deal with. First is the reflectivity of both the glass and the water. Using flash under such circumstances is problematic. Another problem is colors underwater are muted, depending on the depth of the water. (This tends to be more of a problem at destination aquariums than it is with a home fish tank.)
- **Color effects.** This is kind of a catchall for the different tricks point-and-shoot cameras can play with color. Some may offer the ability to mute or pop colors; others may offer the ability to switch or reverse colors or remove all colors but one.
- **Panoramic mode.** This is an interesting feature I'm seeing on more and more point-and-shoot cameras. Even my inexpensive Fuji S2950, a sub $200 camera, has a ridiculously easy to use panoramic function that helps you compose the panorama and stitch them together, no tripod necessary. I also have a Canon G11 and a Fuji X10, and they both have panoramic features that make this type of photography a breeze.

Semi-Automatic/Manual Exposure Modes

As your enthusiasm for controlling the appearance of your point-and-shoot snapshots grows, you may want to explore the typical camera's semi-automatic and manual exposure modes, called Programmed exposure (or Program AE, or some variation), Aperture-priority, Shutter-priority, or Manual exposure (referred to as PASM for short). You can choose these using the mode dial, which I explained in Chapter 3.

- **Program mode (P).** Programmed automation is one of the simpler auto-exposure modes. It determines both shutter speed and lens opening (aperture) for the lighting situation you're facing. It follows an algorithm that begins by emphasizing a fast enough shutter speed to avoid blur from camera shake. Once an appropriate shutter speed is selected, the camera selects a smaller f/stop to increase the depth-of-field (the range in which everything is acceptably sharp). P is a good choice for general lighting conditions, especially when you're more concerned about composition or following action, and leaves you free to worry about things other than exposure. It can produce incorrect exposure when you're dealing with backlighting though (your light source is behind the subject). Later in this chapter I'll show you how to change *metering modes* (the area of the scene that is measured to determine exposure) as a way of dealing with this.

- **Aperture-priority.** You set the aperture (f/stop, lens opening) and the camera chooses the appropriate shutter speed. This is helpful when you need to shoot at a specific lens opening to achieve a certain depth-of-field or for when you want to always shoot at the fastest possible shutter speed and set the lens to its maximum aperture.
- **Shutter-priority.** You set the shutter speed and the camera picks the appropriate aperture. This is useful when shooting at a particular shutter speed is desirable. An example might be if you're trying to blur moving water and need to shoot at a particularly slow shutter speed, or when you want to freeze action using a very high shutter speed.
- **Manual exposure.** You set both the shutter speed and aperture in this mode, giving you full control over both. Some point-and-shoot cameras make using manual settings a bit clumsy, however. It's worth studying your user's manual to learn how to use manual exposure.

Understanding the Exposure Triangle

Because your point-and-shoot camera has automated exposure features, as you begin shooting you may not be concerned with the finer points of exposure right away. However, as you advance, you'll want to learn more about how you can adjust any of the three legs of the *exposure triangle* to improve the overall appearance of your photographs.

There are three primary controls that affect exposure: ISO, shutter speed, and lens opening (f/stop). They work together mutually and reciprocally, so changing one affects the others. While many point-and-shoot cameras offer to take the work out of this, relying on auto ISO and autoexposure can limit your picture-making skills. Taking charge of these settings can lead to better photos once you learn the finer points of each setting and how to take advantage of them.

Shutter Speed

The shutter speed setting determines how long the shutter remains open, exposing the imaging sensor to light. Your choice of shutter speed helps freeze motion (using fast shutter speeds, from 1/125th to 1/1,000th second or briefer), prevent blur from camera movement, or show movement through the use of the blurring emphasized by slower shutter speeds (from about 1/60th second to 1 full second or longer). Shutter speed also plays a role in how fast your camera's continuous shooting speed works because the longer the shutter takes to capture an image, the less time the camera has between consecutive shots. With a 1/2-second shutter speed, for example, it's obviously impossible to capture more than two pictures per second.

Showing Action

Sometimes showing action involves freezing motion. To do this, make sure you're using the fastest shutter speed you reasonably can. As a rough rule of thumb, a shutter speed of 1/500th of a second will freeze many athletes, whereas faster speeds may be necessary to freeze a tennis racket or baseball bat. Although 1/500th of a second may be the limit for low-end point-and-shoot cameras, better quality models may be capable of shutter speeds hitting 1/2,000th or even 1/4,000th of a second.

Avoiding Blur from Camera Shake

The longer the shutter remains open, the more camera movement can contribute to image blur. Keep in mind, too, that the more you zoom in (using a longer focal length, say, the 100mm setting instead of the 28mm wide-angle setting) the more any camera movement is magnified. With many of today's super zoom point-and-shoot cameras with effective zoom settings of 420mm or more, it's quite possible to overwhelm the ability of your camera's image stabilization system to compensate for camera shake. Some cameras will warn you if you're using such a slow shutter speed/long lens combination that camera shake is a problem.

If your camera doesn't have that warning, there's an old rule that relies on the reciprocal of the focal length to determine the correct shutter speed. This "rule" (it's more of a rough guideline actually) says if you're using a 250mm lens (an effective focal length many point-and-shoot cameras offer), you should be using a shutter speed of at least 1/250th of a second. Image stabilization can probably give you at least two "stops" worth of compensation (a "stop" is a standard unit of measure in photography); that means 1/60th of a second is the slowest shutter speed you should try to hand-hold your camera when at that focal length.

Creative Blur

Intentional blur can be an interesting and creative tool. Suppose you're photographing a dancer and you want to convey a sense of how fast he's moving. Choosing a moderately slow shutter speed can blur his arms and legs while leaving the rest of him sharp enough to be recognizable. It will take a little experimentation to find the best shutter speed, and you should plan on taking many photos to maximize your chances of success, but this technique can produce some beautiful images. (See Figure 4.3.)

Another useful approach is to photograph the reflection of fall leaves in the water and use a slow enough shutter speed that the movement of the leaves

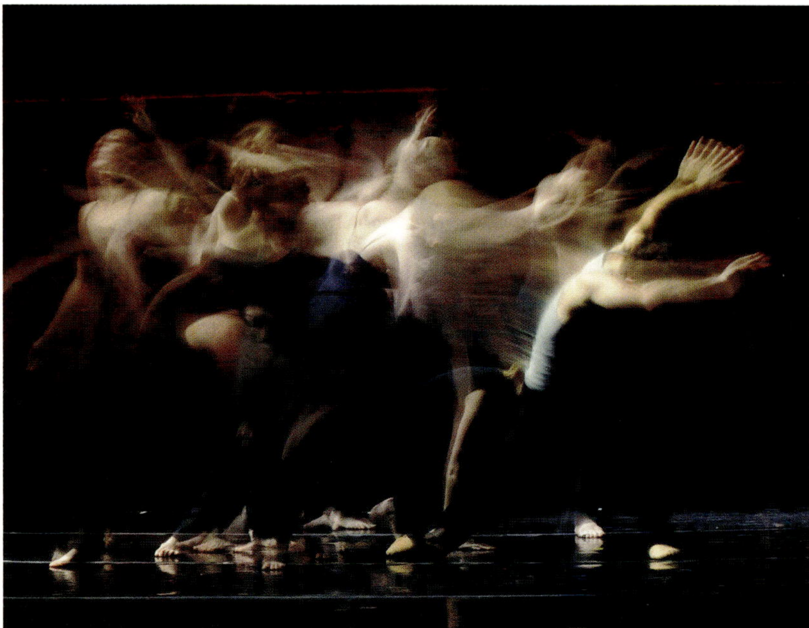

Figure 4.3 Blur can be used to create a more interesting image.

from wind causes the reflections to blur together in a mélange of colors. Mount the camera on a tripod so the elements of the shot such as the shoreline or tree line stay sharp.

Panning

One of the neat things you can do with a camera and a slow shutter speed is pan the camera while making a long exposure (a tripod is helpful). The idea is to keep the camera as steady as possible when it comes to vertical movement while maintaining a slow but steady pivot (it's best to keep your lower body still and make the most extreme turn from the waist that you can). Check to see if your camera offers multiple image stabilization settings. If it does, at least one of them should be designed to help you with the panning movement. Some cameras require shutting off image stabilization entirely when panning; your camera manual will alert you if this is the case. (See Figure 4.4.)

Lens Opening/Aperture/f/stop

Our next member of the exposure triangle is the size of the lens opening, usually measured in f/stops. This affects the quantity of light striking the imaging sensor. It's kind of counter intuitive; the smaller the f/stop, the larger the lens

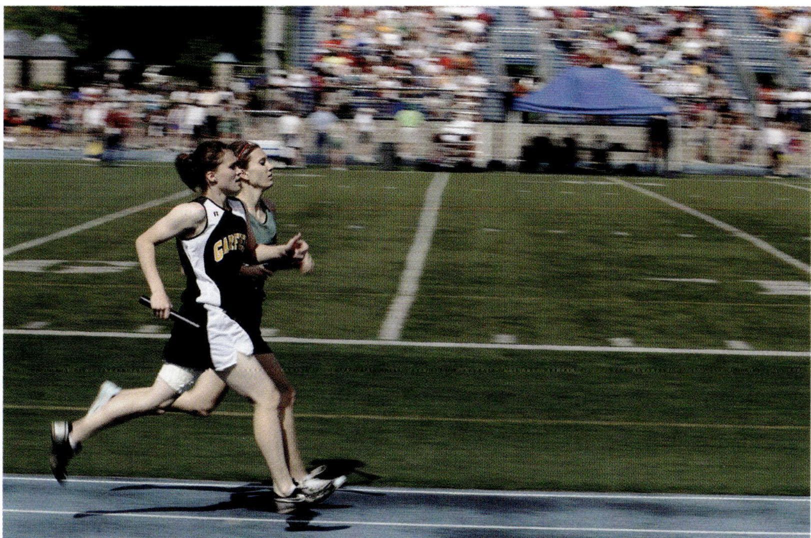

Figure 4.4 It's easy to pan even the least sophisticated point-and-shoot camera to follow action and produce images like this one.

opening. An f/stop of f/4 is twice as large an opening as an f/stop of f/5.6. (f/stops travel in a base 2 logarithmic progression, a fact I enjoy sharing with my photography students since it terrifies them to find out photography can involve math.) Your choice of lens opening does more than admit light to the sensor though. It also helps you exercise a great deal of creative control.

Depth-of-Field

Depth-of-field refers to the apparent depth of sharpness within an image. It's controlled by the size of the lens opening, with smaller lens openings producing greater depth-of-field. Unfortunately, point-and-shoot cameras are a bit limited when it comes to managing depth-of-field. This is because the relationship between the size of the lens and the small imaging sensors these cameras have makes depth-of-field extremes difficult.

Selective Focus

This is a popular portrait technique that calls for a wide-open lens (large lens opening, small f/stop) and a longer focal length in order to keep the subject sharp and the background out of focus. It's difficult to do well with point-and-shoot cameras since their longer focal lengths tend to have small maximum apertures. Getting closer to your subject will help, as will using your camera's portrait mode setting. (See Figure 4.5.)

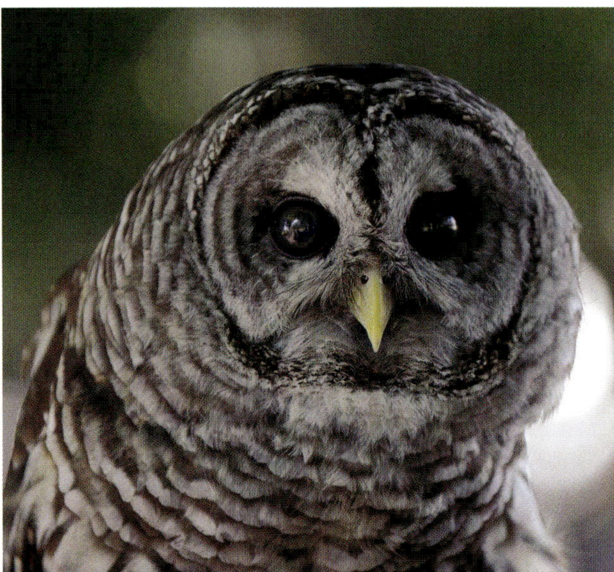

Figure 4.5
Using your camera's lens opening can show a sharp image throughout the entire image or just selectively to concentrate the viewer's eye on the main subject.

EXPOSURE COMPENSATION

Your camera probably has an exposure compensation setting, frequently marked with a + and – symbol. When you select exposure compensation, the camera will add more exposure to the next shot or series of shots when you dial in the + direction, making the image brighter; or reduce exposure and make the image darker when you dial toward the – symbol. Exposure compensation can also be specified separately for electronic flash pictures.

ISO Sensitivity

This setting controls the imaging sensor's sensitivity to light. The lower the ISO setting, the less sensitive to light the sensor is, requiring a larger lens opening or slower shutter speed or both. A general rule of thumb is that the lowest ISO setting produces the cleanest images with the least amount of visual noise or graininess. Some point-and-shoot cameras will have an ideal ISO setting and extended ISO options beyond the ideal setting and past the normal highest setting. These extreme settings often diminish image quality. There are a couple of things to consider when setting ISO sensitivity, discussed next.

Noise

The higher ISO setting you choose, the more the imaging sensor has to boost its sensitivity light. But the harder the sensor has to work, the more heat it generates. This heat can cause the sensor's photosites to misinterpret data. The result is a problem known as "noise."

Noise can seriously degrade the quality of your image. The primary cause of noise is using a high ISO setting; it can also happen when you underexpose an image and then try to fix it in an image-editing program. When selecting an ISO setting, go with the lowest ISO setting you can (provided it gives the best quality image for your camera) that still permits you to use the f/stop and shutter speed you need to achieve the photograph you want.

Extended ISO

Some cameras will offer an extended ISO setting or settings. These extreme settings often push the camera's limits and serve as emergency-only options, as they produce somewhat grainy results (see Figure 4.6). In some cases, these

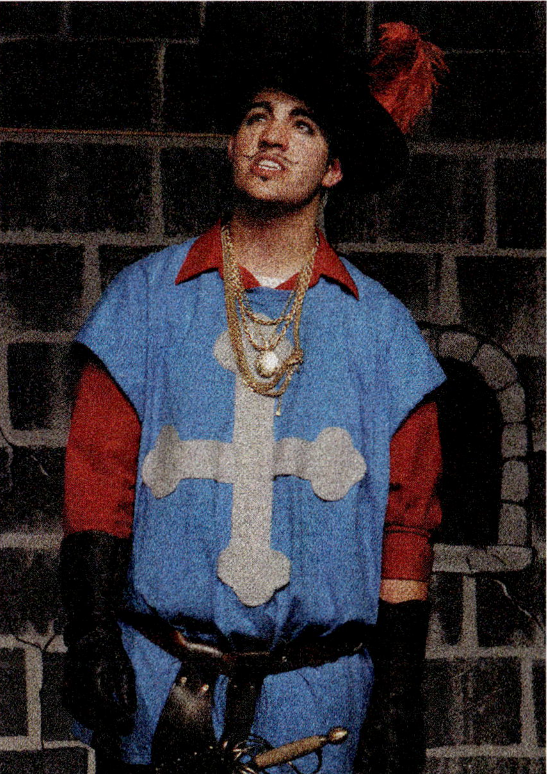

Figure 4.6
Extreme ISO settings can result in image noise in your photographs.

settings are only possible at a lower resolution; in others, the extreme ISOs are achieved by manipulation (the camera shoots at its highest or lowest ISO, deliberately under or overexposing the image and then compensating via in-camera digital processing). You can do the same thing yourself in a photo-editing program such as Photoshop.

Metering Modes

Your point-and-shoot camera may give you some control over the metering mode used to determine exposure. Metering mode governs the part of the frame that is measured when calculating the appropriate f/stop, shutter speed, or ISO setting to use. Your choices might include:

- **Evaluative metering.** Evaluative metering (often referred to by other names such as "Digital ESP" or "Matrix metering," depending on the manufacturer) is the camera maker's best effort at producing a superior exposure metering system. The camera looks at many different zones or areas of the frame, and then compares its readings with a "canned" database of image types to choose an exposure that worked for that kind of image in the past. Or the camera may divide the image into specific zones and give priority to those most typically used for important picture elements, such as the foreground.
- **Center-weighted metering.** In this mode, the exposure meter emphasizes a zone in the center of the frame to calculate exposure. A certain percentage of the exposure, usually about 75 percent, is based on that central area, and the remaining exposure is based on the rest of the frame. The theory, here, is that, for most pictures, the main subject will be located in the center.
- **Spot metering.** Spot metering measures a very small area of the frame, usually amounting to only a few percent of the overall image, and calculates exposure based only on that part. Spot metering is useful in any situation in which you want to individually measure the light reflecting from light, midtone, or dark areas of your subject, or any combination of areas. Most point-and-shooters won't use Spot metering much, but as you advance in your skills, you might want to explore exposure techniques described in online tutorials and in a variety of books.

Autofocus

Proper focus is one of the key requirements for an acceptable image. In fact, research conducted by one-hour photo printers has consistently shown that "out of focus" is the number one reason photos are rejected. Your camera can set focus precisely and accurately and yet the resulting image can be unacceptably soft due to other factors.

Let's look at some of the things we have to get right in order to achieve "sharp" images:

- **Proper lens focusing.** The lens needs to be focused precisely on the area of the image the photographer wants in focus. The camera can only do what the photographer instructs it to. If the focusing sensor is pointed at the wrong object, then even though the camera did its job properly, the photographer ends up unhappy with the results.
- **Depth-of-field.** Depth-of-field refers to the apparent sharpness throughout the image area from foreground through middle ground through background. A photograph with great depth-of-field will appear sharp throughout the entire image. A photograph with shallow depth-of-field may only appear sharp at a small point in the image.
- **Contrast.** Images with good contrast appear sharper than images that don't have good contrast. In fact, in digital photography, sharpness is really determined by edge contrast.
- **Lighting.** It's easy to think that the key to photographic lighting is to get enough light to make a proper exposure, but this is only a starting point for good photography. Both a light source's direction and quality can play a role in apparent image sharpness.
- **Shooting technique.** Taking pictures is a bit more complicated than you might think. Your shooting technique can lead to sharper or softer photos, depending on how you hold and operate your camera. Besides making sure you have a fast enough shutter speed dialed in and your camera's image stabilization turned on, you still need to hold the camera steady and squeeze the shutter gently. Getting sharp photographs calls for more than proper focusing. One of the most important components is using the proper shooting technique as shown here. Notice how Lisa is cradling the camera in her hands and bracing it against her forehead. This provides greater stability than holding the camera at arm's length and composing the image with the LCD screen (sadly, many camera viewfinders do not give an accurate view of what the lens sees, making this technique less effective). Also, see how she braces her elbows on the table. This is a deliberate move to further reduce camera shake (See Figure 4.7.)

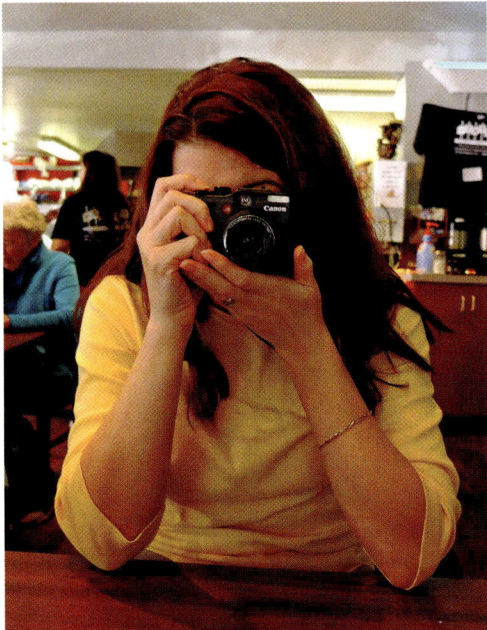

Figure 4.7
Getting sharp photographs calls for proper shooting technique.

Configuring Your Camera's Autofocus System

Most point-and-shoot digital cameras offer multiple autofocus options, including a feature called *focus assist*, which most often illuminates an LED lamp on the front of the camera to provide more light for the focusing system to use. Some cameras include a magnification feature that enlarges the center of the frame on the LCD, so you can fine-tune focus manually. The most common autofocus modes are as follows:

- **Single shot autofocus.** Single shot autofocus mode attempts to lock focus on whatever subject the focusing sensor is pointed. Once the lens locks focus, the shutter trips and the picture is made. If the lens is unable to lock focus, the camera generally won't fire (some cameras may offer a custom function that lets you turn this control off).
- **Continuous autofocus.** In this mode, the lens continues to focus even after it has achieved focus on the subject. This is an effective mode for sports and action photography since it lets you track a moving subject and keep it in focus, provided the camera's autofocus technology can keep up with the movement. Normally straight-line movements are easier for the camera to follow than zig-zag type action.

- **Manual focus.** Many point-and-shoot cameras offer a manual focus setting, but few of them are actually easy to focus this way. This option is most useful when the camera is mounted on a tripod or some other stable platform and the subject is stationary, so the focus can be dialed in precisely without the camera or subject moving out of focus.
- **Face recognition.** This is a newer option for point-and-shoot cameras and a particularly useful one too. Face recognition is sometimes offered in two different versions. The basic face recognition is good for identifying faces in general and makes it much easier on the shooter when photographing situations in which the primary concern is getting people in focus. A second version (usually called "face recognition or registration") is more specific. Here, the camera is taught to remember certain faces, so it can make getting those faces in focus a priority over any other faces in the shot. This is perfect for making sure the camera focuses on your grandchild and not her annoying aunt Betty by mistake. In order to take advantage of face recognition you have to register the individual's face with the camera (check your owner's manual to learn how). Depending on the camera and how good a job you did of registering the person's face, it can recognize someone even if their face isn't turned to perfectly face the camera. Some cameras can recognize when a subject is smiling and trip the shutter at that point.

Your best bet is to anticipate the kind of photography you're going to do and set your camera accordingly. If you're shooting your child's birthday party, face recognition, face registration (of your daughter and spouse's faces), and continuous autofocus will probably give you the best results. If you're on vacation and photographing the scenery, turn off face recognition and rely on either single shot autofocus or manual focus with focus assist (especially if you're using a tripod or some other device to keep your camera stationary). See the shooting tips section of this book for more ideas on tweaking your camera for specific shoots.

Here's my old family recipe for sharp images:

- **ISO.** Make sure your ISO is set high enough to let you choose an effective shutter speed (1/125th without IS; if IS is on then you can drop down to 1/60th).
- **Autofocus.** Choose the autofocus setting you prefer.
- **Face recognition.** If your shoot includes human beings, turn face recognition on. (See Figure 4.8.)

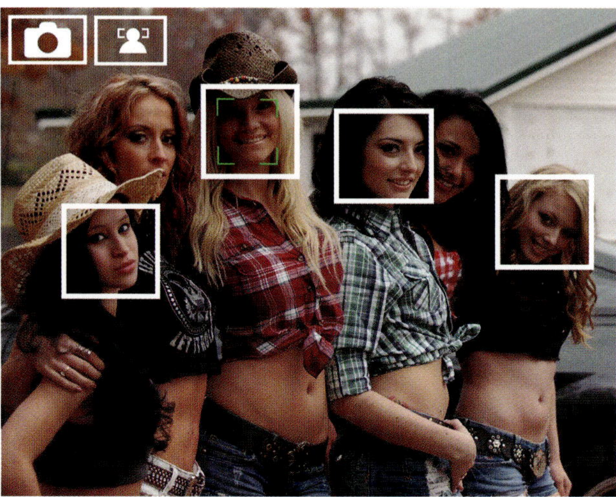

Figure 4.8
Face recognition is the latest in autofocus technology.

- **Depth-of-field.** Try to operate your camera with your lens set to less than your maximum aperture to gain improved depth-of-field.
- **Lighting.** If possible, position your lens at a right angle to the light source. This will cause the light to track across your subject. Side lighting is great for showing detail and will also help your images appear sharper.
- **Keep it steady.** Try to hold your camera as steady as possible and squeeze the shutter as gently as possible.

Using Your Zoom Lens

With very few exceptions, point-and-shoot cameras come with zoom lenses rather than fixed focal length, non-zooming lenses. This makes sense for most shooters since you can't change lenses on your point-and-shoot cameras and often don't like or don't want to carry around front mounting lens adapters. Since many people prefer the point-and-shoot format because they want a small, compact, and easy-to-use camera, carrying accessory lenses would defeat the purpose of buying a point-and-shoot camera.

One thing to be aware of when using a point-and-shoot camera's zoom lens is that camera makers often promote two types of zoom function—optical and digital. While both of these are useful, there are important differences between the two.

Optical Zoom

The camera's optical zoom is the actual glass optics that physically zooms in and out over a specific focal length range (such as 24mm-120mm). The camera's optical zoom can be thought of as a "true" zoom requiring no digital tricks to create the image.

Most point-and-shoot cameras utilize a power zoom, which extends and retracts the zoom via a lever that's usually part of the shutter release button collar. On rare occasions a camera maker may choose to provide a more traditional zoom approach, such as with the Fuji X10, which requires you to manually twist the lens barrel to zoom in and out (and turn the camera on for that matter).

Generally, manipulating the optical zoom will have minimal effect on your image quality. Although a lens may perform slightly better (and by slightly I mean barely noticeable under normal shooting situations) at one end of the zoom range, no matter where you are in the zoom range, the lens's performance will be pretty consistent. That's not quite true with the next zoom version.

Digital Zoom

Many point-and-shoot cameras will describe their zoom range something like this: 10X optical/4X digital zoom. The 4X represents a multiplier of a maximum of four times whatever focal length the optical zoom is set to. If you're shooting with the lens set to 100mm and employ the digital zoom at maximum capability, you end up with the equivalent of a 400mm lens.

With the optical zoom, you're merely operating the lens at an existing focal length. The digital zoom on the other hand effectively takes the image created by the 100mm optic and crops it down by a factor of four and then enlarges the crop to the camera's normal image size (using an interpolation algorithm to account for the extra pixels). This is comparable to creating an image with the lens set to 100mm and then cropping it down in an image-editing program and then uprezzing the file to match the normal file size for images from your camera. The problem with this technique is that you usually lose a fair amount of image quality because no algorithm is as capable as a camera lens.

Exploring Drive Modes

Your camera offers several options for controlling the picture-making process. The drive mode controls what happens when you press and hold the shutter button. It's safe to assume that pressing the shutter button somehow results in a photo being made, but there are several different ways of getting that done.

Just about every mid-range point-and-shoot camera offers a full set of drive modes; how you access these modes varies from camera to camera. In fact, many cameras don't group all the options usually thought of as drive modes with the same control. Let's look at some of the common drive modes and discuss where they can be found:

- **Single shot.** Plain and simple. Push the shutter button and take a picture. This is usually represented by a small rectangle. Some cameras have a button, arrow pad, or rocker pad that lets you activate the drive modes panel and select this option. Other cameras will have you navigate the shooting menu system.
- **Continuous shot.** Back in the old days, we used to call this a motor drive. From a technology point of view that term is no longer correct, so we tend to go with continuous shot or sequential shooting mode or some other phrase that implies the camera will keep taking pictures as long as the shutter button is held down.
- **High-speed/Low-speed continuous shot.** Some cameras may offer you a choice between the camera's fastest possible frame rate and a slower frame rate. More advanced point-and-shoot cameras may even offer a super-high-speed mode that increases the frame rate to incredibly fast speeds (10 frames a second or faster) at the cost of resolution. (See Figure 4.9.)
- **Self-timer.** Most point-and-shoot cameras have at least one and usually two self-timer options. There tends to be a shorter option (about two seconds) and a longer option (about 10 seconds). These may be accessed via a button or pad or through the camera's menu system (usually the shooting menu). Some cameras allow you to fire off a series of shots (2 to 9) after the delay has elapsed, increasing your chances of getting a photo in which no eyes are closed.

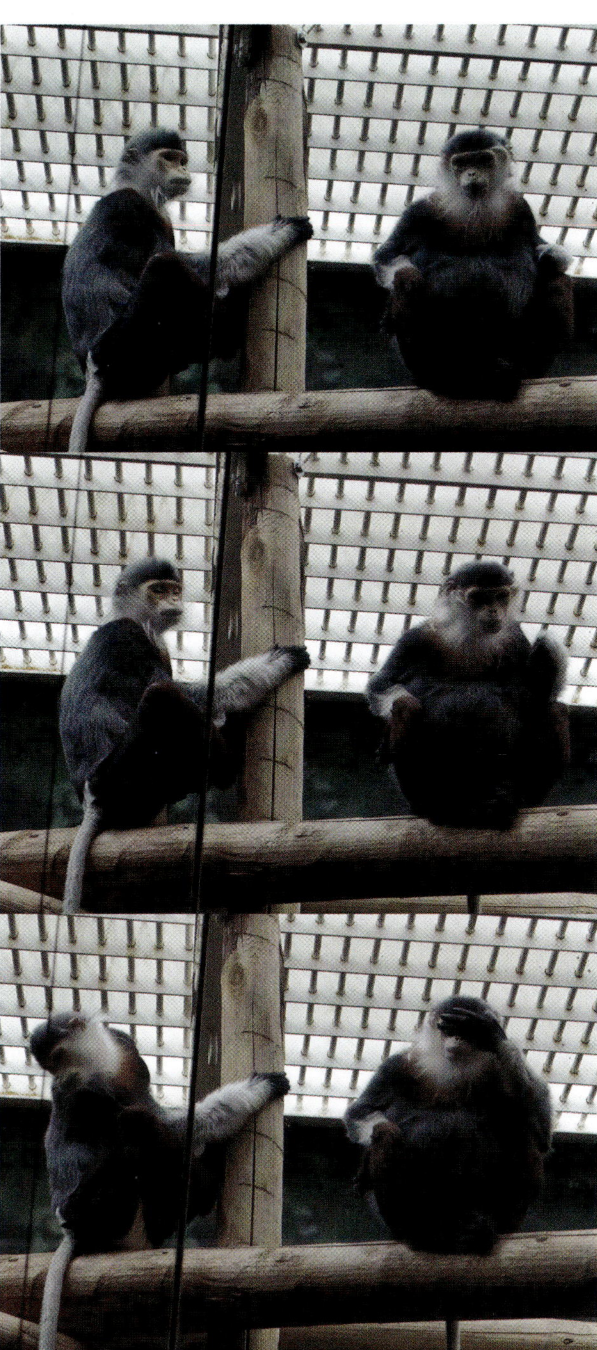

Figure 4.9
Many mid- and high-end point-and-shoot cameras provide high-speed modes capable of 7 fps or faster.

Flash Controls

Rare is the point-and-shoot camera that doesn't have a built-in flash of some kind. These small light sources serve in a pinch, but also at a cost. They drain your camera's batteries more rapidly than normal operation; they tend to produce harsh direct lighting; and they can be prone to "red-eye," that otherworldly glow in your subject's eyes.

Still, they do serve as a portable, easy-to-use light source, particularly when you just need some extra light for fill flash or times when you have no other choice. Your point-and-shoot camera does offer a reasonable amount of control over your built-in flash in several different ways.

If you need to use flash often, or shoot a lot of video, then buying a small video light can be a great idea. Many of these lights cost less than $25 and can do wonders for video or supplemental lighting. An added advantage to using them for still photography is that you can use them off-camera, vastly improving the quality of your lighting. You don't need to do anything special as far as your camera is concerned either. It will white balance the light automatically (at least if you're using auto white balance) and expose automatically too (provided you're using autoexposure).

Built-In Flash Controls

Your camera's built-in flash unit most likely offers several different options, depending on your shooting needs. There are basic controls that determine whether the flash will fire; options for dealing with red-eye; and, on many cameras, the ability to dial down or boost flash output as needed.

Here are the most common electronic flash controls:

- **Off.** The flash doesn't fire under any circumstances.
- **On.** Flash attempts (provided its capacitor is charged enough) to fire every time the shutter button is pressed.
- **Auto.** Depending on the situation, the camera determines when the flash fires.
- **Red-eye reduction.** Many recent cameras offer what's known as "red-eye reduction mode." Red-eye is caused by light from your camera's flash reflecting off your subject's pupils and bouncing back into your lens (it's actually lens flare). This is why you see pro photographers working to get their flash units farther away from their cameras than any built-in flash unit is capable of.

- **Flash exposure compensation.** Most point-and-shoot cameras offer some form of flash exposure compensation. This is useful for times when you want your flash to help out but not dominate. Another reason for this control is for those times when your subject is darker or lighter than what the camera considers "normal." In this situation, you can dial in extra flash output or reduced flash output to get the proper illumination.

White Balance/Color Adjustments

Digital cameras need to be white balanced for best color reproduction. "White balancing" is simply telling your camera what pure white is. Once it knows this, it can pretty much get other colors right. Your camera will offer you some way of controlling its white balance, but if you're not really interested in this level of control, you can just set your camera to Auto White Balance.

If you do want to exercise more control, your camera will offer you a number of white balance options, including user-defined white balance.

Your white balance options normally include:

- **AWB.** Auto White Balance. The camera evaluates the lighting and chooses the appropriate white balance. This setting usually does a good job in most situations, and if you don't know much about photography or aren't particularly concerned about critical color accuracy, leave it on this setting.
- **Daylight.** This setting is for when your main light source is the sun (indoors or outdoors).
- **Cloudy.** If it's a cloudy or overcast day, then this is the best choice. Sunlight filtered through clouds tends to be a bit bluer than straight sunlight.
- **Tungsten.** This is a type of incandescent lighting that is considerably "cooler" (bluish) than daylight. If you shoot with your camera set to this white balance and tungsten lighting does not illuminate your scene, your images will end up with a bluish cast to them.
- **Fluorescent lighting (white).** Fluorescent lights come in many different types, including variations on "white" and "daylight." This setting is for use under the white version.
- **Fluorescent lighting (daylight).** This setting is for use under the daylight version.

- **Flash.** This white balance setting compensates for the light from a flash unit, whether it's a built-in flash or an accessory strobe. These lights tend to have a little blue to their output.
- **Underwater.** This setting white balances the camera for underwater photography. This is a nice option if you plan to use your camera in an underwater housing for snorkeling or scuba diving since light rays act different underwater than above it. This setting does not seal it any better or make it waterproof in any way. You still need a special housing to use it underwater unless it is specifically sold as an underwater camera. (See Figure 4.10.)
- **Custom white balance.** You can set your own white balance for the camera to follow. In some cameras you do this by photographing a white sheet of paper or a gray card under the light you're shooting in. Other cameras let you dial in a specific color temperature. (Color temperature in degrees Kelvin is how photographers evaluate the color of the light. You'd use this feature if you had some type of unusual lighting and were aware of the light's color temperature.)

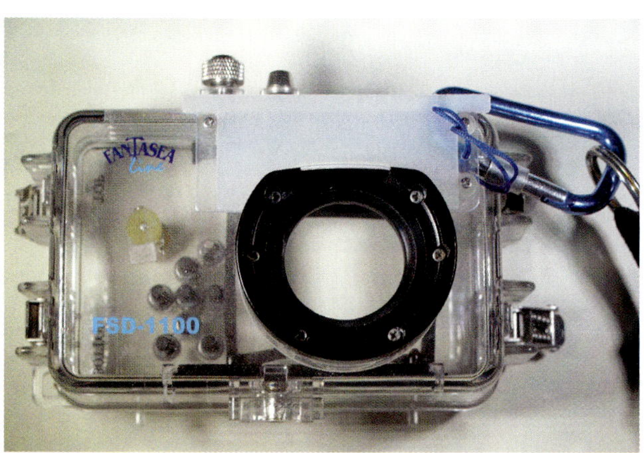

Figure 4.10
Cameras designed to be underwater in a protective housing often have an underwater white balance to produce more accurate color.

Chapter 5

Special Features

Camera makers can add features without increasing the size or cost of the camera by developing special features via software and then implementing them throughout their camera line. Back in the film camera days, special features had to be implemented via mechanical changes, a much more expensive process. If you wanted faster continuous shooting ("motor drive"), for example, you had to build a faster motor. Today, all that's required is a more sensitive sensor and speedier digital signal processing engine. It's still "hardware," in a sense, but the improvements come at the electronics level, not from nuts-and-bolts.

Depending on what camera you have, there will probably be some special options you can take advantage of. Currently, the most common appear to be color effects, panoramic photography, and high dynamic range (HDR) photography, along with movie making.

Multi-Image Special Features

Quality point-and-shoot cameras often offer a set of features based on the idea of creating, modifying, or combining a group of images rather than just one photo. The list of features includes a number of possibilities.

Bracketing is a process of creating one image at what seems to be the best settings and then creating two or more images at slightly different settings to hedge your bets. Other multi-shot special features are designed to take several images and combine them in a way that creates an improved image.

- **Exposure bracketing.** Most point-and-shoot cameras offer some form of exposure bracketing. Often you can decide how many extra images it creates and how extreme the exposure variations are (that is, the size of the increment between shots, say, half a stop, a full stop, or some other value). Normally you find the bracketing setting in the camera's shooting menu, but some cameras provide access via the drive button instead. Depending

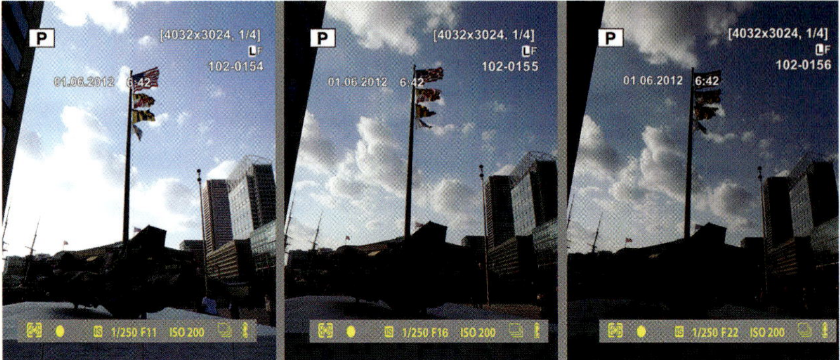

Figure 5.1 Auto bracketing provides a tool for maximizing your chances of getting the best possible exposure.

on your camera, you may still need to trip the shutter three, five, or seven times (depending on how many exposures you want with each scene) to get a full set. Other cameras will create the images automatically, shooting a sequence of pictures with a single press of the shutter release (see Figure 5.1).

- **White balance bracket.** This is a less common option, but one still found on many cameras. Here the camera creates multiple images, each with a different white balance setting. You may be able to specify the color bias, say, along the blue/amber axis or green/magenta axis. Many cameras take a single shot, and save several versions, one at each color balance setting. Depending on your camera, you'll probably access this control either via the shooting menu controls or the camera's drive controls.
- **ISO bracket.** If you want to keep the same shutter speed and aperture, but still want to bracket your exposures, you can use ISO bracketing instead. Auto ISO bracketing takes three shots, each at a different ISO setting. Cameras offering this option usually create the three images on one shutter press.
- **Film simulation bracket.** Another popular option for digital cameras is the ability to simulate the looks created by different types of film (the stuff photographers used back in the days before digital cameras). Certain film types were very popular back in the day, so camera makers have incorporated different film profiles to create similar looks. Common film simulations include popular slide (transparency) films such as Fuji Velvia or negative films such as Provia. Another version of this is to offer a choice between "Standard," "Chrome," and "Print Film." If your camera offers a Film Simulation Bracket option, it will create multiple images using each film style.

- **Dynamic range bracket.** Some higher-end point-and-shoot cameras offer a *dynamic range* boost (that is, the range of tones from dark to light that are captured) to help manage high-contrast lighting. If your camera offers this feature, it will usually create three images with one press of the shutter button going through its range of dynamic range options in full f/stop variations. This is another control that's usually accessed via the shooting menu or the drive button.
- **High dynamic range (HDR) capture.** This is another way of extending the apparent tonal range of an image. HDR photography recognizes the limitations of the digital camera sensor and compensates by recording several images and merging them for a higher quality final image. The process involves shooting one image to expose the brightest area of the scene (highlight) and another for the darkest areas (shadows). Sometimes HDR photography will include a third frame for the mid-tones as well. It's important that the camera use the same lens opening (f/stop) for each image in order to keep depth-of-field the same. The camera or photographer will usually change the shutter speed, ISO, or both to accomplish this. The camera will then merge the images together for the finished file. Generally, you get the best results from using the camera on a tripod or some other stable platform when making this kind of image since it's important that the image be exactly the same as the other images with the exception of the exposure information. (See Figure 5.2.)
- **Best frame capture.** Your camera may offer some kind of "Best Frame Capture" option. If you pick this option, the camera will fire a burst of images and save only the one that it deems to be sharpest, best exposed, or matching other criteria. Some can even detect whether a human subject's eyes are closed, and reject those in favor of one where the eyes are open.
- **Panoramic images.** It's becoming more common for point-and-shoot cameras to offer some kind of panoramic assistance feature. One camera I work with (a Fuji S2950) lets you choose between a two-shot and a three-shot panorama. This camera makes actually shooting the multi-shot sequence surprisingly easy. Just press the shutter and then maneuver the camera so that a small plus (+) sign fits into a cutout of the same sign. Once done, the camera stitches the images together and displays the final panorama. My Fuji X10 offers a different approach that gives a full 360-degree panorama. With this camera you set the camera to the appropriate mode, press the shutter, and slowly turn while keeping the camera level (a guide line is there to help). Once done, the camera stitches the images together and plays the finished shot across the LCD screen for your review. The Canon G15 I'm using for this book also has a panorama assist feature that, while perhaps not as elegant, still makes creating a panoramic photo pretty easy. (See Figure 5.3.)

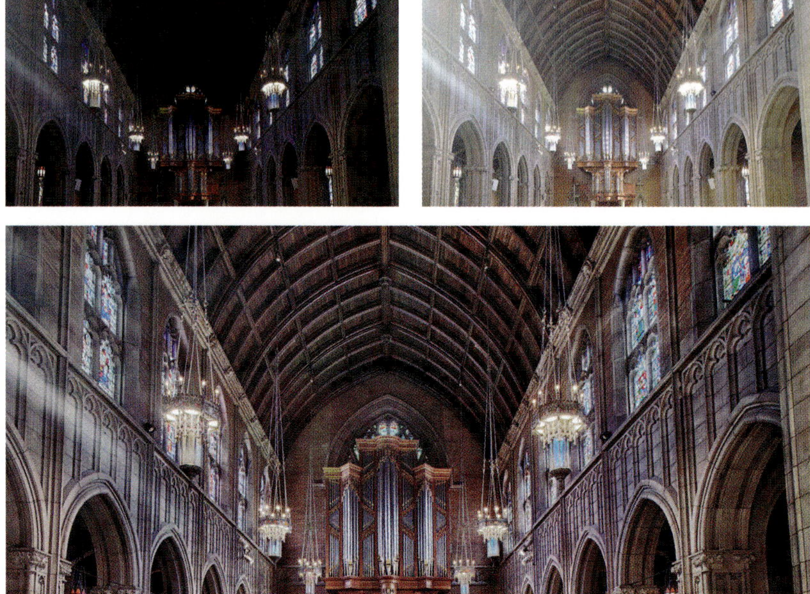

Figure 5.2 HDR photography combines an underexposure (top left) and overexposure (top right) to produce a final image with an extremely long range of tones (bottom).

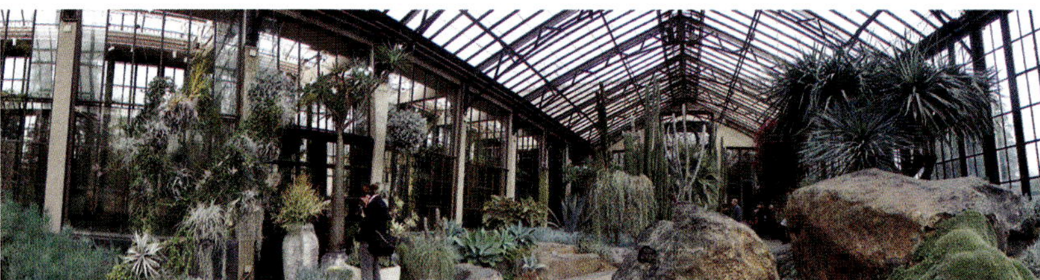

Figure 5.3 Panoramic assist seems to be one of the most common special features in current point-and-shoot cameras. While the approach varies from camera to camera, it does make it much easier to create panoramas.

Color Effects

Color effects are another popular class of special features available on many of today's point-and-shoot digital cameras, providing a wide variety of things you can do to manipulate image color to achieve unusual looking or striking photos.

Back in the film days, color manipulation required a lot of external work. Your film choice, filter availability, gels availability (gels are sheets of a colored gelatin material that you would place over your flash head or studio lights to provide a color cast to the light), and other tricks (including processing and development tricks) would help you create a different color look for your photo. This process involved a lot of trial and error, often wasted time, and also called for an investment in a lot of accessories. Today, we can play with color all we want, just with the tools our cameras give us. It's a heck of an improvement! Here are some of the color options our point-and-shoot cameras might offer:

- **Sepia.** Sepia toning refers to a light brownish tone that makes the photo "old timey." (See Figure 5.4.)

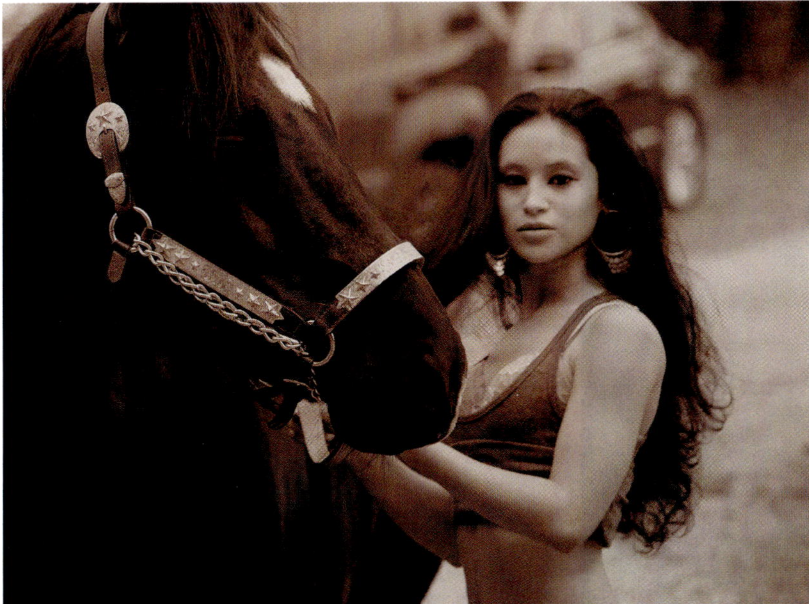

Figure 5.4 Sepia-toned images present an "old timey" photo look.

- **Black-and-white.** Often black-and-white photos can be more expressive than color images. Finding a point-and-shoot camera that will shoot in black-and-white mode isn't difficult at all, and a good number of them also offer the ability to simulate using a color contrast filter. Color contrast filters (usually red, green, or blue) are used to increase or change contrast in black-and-white images.
- **Vivid/Pop color.** This setting adds a lot of saturation to colors, making them especially vivid and rich. When used with subjects that have a lot of bright colors, the effect can be dramatic. Duller subjects gain a more "normal" appearance (try using this setting on an overcast day to see what I mean).
- **Skin tones.** Some cameras will record skin tones differently (lighter or darker or perhaps smoother) than normal camera settings will.
- **Vivid single color.** This option lets you choose one color to accentuate. A nice option, for example, is being able to have the camera spice up the color blue to add life to skies in landscape photos.
- **Color select.** Lets you choose one color to record, leaving the rest of the colors in the image to record in black-and-white. (See Figure 5.5.)
- **Color swap.** Lets you choose one color to record, and then lets you swap that color with another color. (See Figure 5.6.)
- **Toy camera.** Produces images like you might get with a Diana or Holga "plastic" camera, with vignetted corners, image blurring, and bright, saturated colors.
- **Posterization.** This option produces a vivid, high-contrast image that emphasizes the primary colors (as shown in Figure 5.7), or in black-and-white, with a reduced number of tones, creating a poster effect.

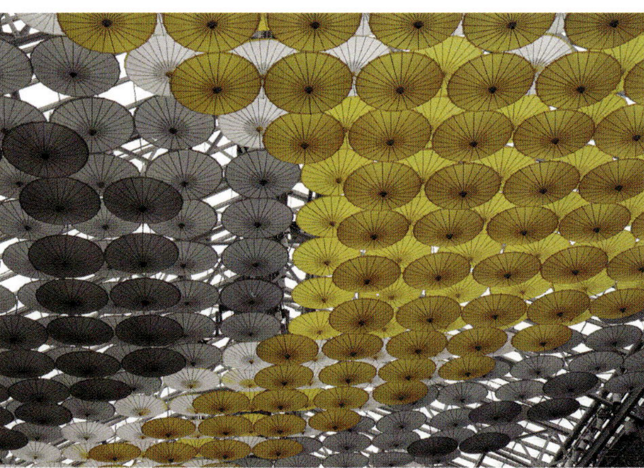

Figure 5.5
Color select lets you isolate one color from your photo while converting all other colors to grayscale.

- **Retro photo.** Adds a faded photo look to the image, with sepia overtones.
- **Soft high key.** Produces bright images.
- **High-contrast monochrome.** Converts the image to black-and-white and boosts the contrast to give a stark look to the image.
- **Soft focus.** Creates a soft, blurry effect.

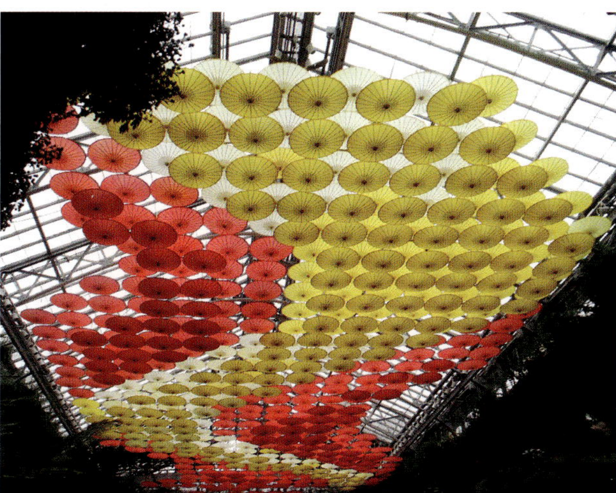

Figure 5.6 With color swap you can replace one color with another.

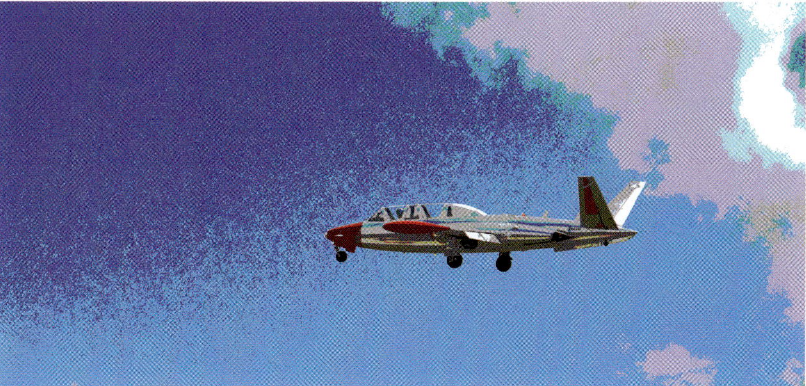

Figure 5.7 Posterization creates an image with a reduced number of tones.

- **Rich-tone monochrome.** Also uses HDR processes to create a long-gradation image from three consecutive exposures.
- **Miniature.** You select the area to be rendered in sharp focus. The effect is similar to the tilt-shift look used to photograph craft models. (See Figure 5.8.)

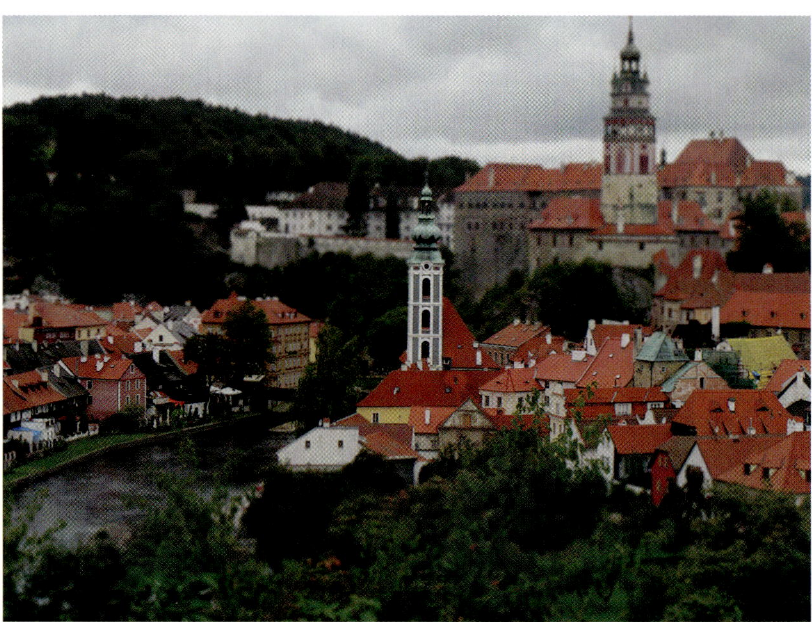

Figure 5.8 The miniature effect uses limited depth-of-field to create a special look.

Shooting Video

Point-and-shoot cameras have had video capture capabilities for many years. But only in the last few years has standard HD or full HD been possible. Your tiny pocket-sized point-and-shoot model just might outperform modestly priced digital video camcorders. There are a number of different things to consider when planning a video shoot, and when possible, a shooting script and storyboard can help you produce a higher quality video.

Use a Shooting Script/Storyboards

A shooting script is nothing more than a coordinated plan that covers both audio and video and provides order and structure for your video. A detailed script will cover what types of shots you're going after, what dialogue you're going to use, audio effects, transitions, and graphics. A storyboard is a series of photos or sketches/drawings that help you visualize locations, placement of actors/actresses, props, and furniture. It also helps show how you want to frame or compose a shot. (See Figure 5.9.)

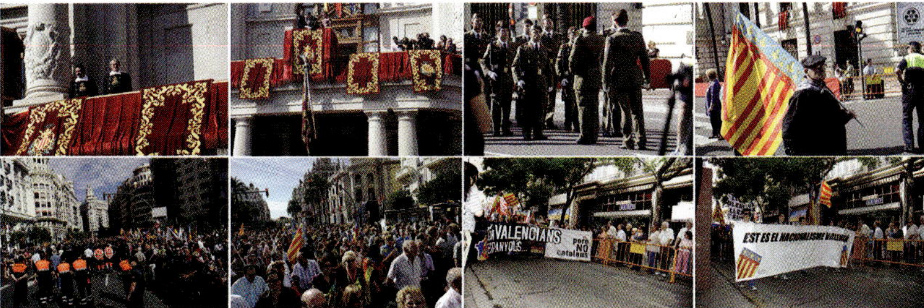

Figure 5.9 A storyboard can help you plan a better video.

Advance a Story

A lot of the work will come after you shoot, when your video is assembled using a movie-editing program like iMovie or Windows Movie Maker. Audio and video should always be advancing the story. While it's okay to let the camera linger from time to time, it should only be for a compelling reason and only briefly. It only takes a second or two for an establishing shot to impart the necessary information, and the same goes for a dramatic stare. Provide variety too. Change camera angles and perspectives often and never leave a static scene on the screen for a long period of time.

Keep Transitions Basic

Fancy transitions that involve exotic "wipes," dissolves, or cross fades take too long for the average viewer and make your video ponderous. Save dissolves to show the passage of time (it's a cinematic convention that viewers are used to and understand).

Composition

Movie shooting calls for careful composition, and, in the case of HD video format, that composition must be framed by the 16:9 horizontal aspect ratio of the format. Some subjects, such as basketball players and tall buildings, lend themselves to vertical compositions. But movies are shown in horizontal format only. So if you're interviewing a local basketball star, you can end up with a worst-case situation like the one shown in Figure 5.10. You really can't

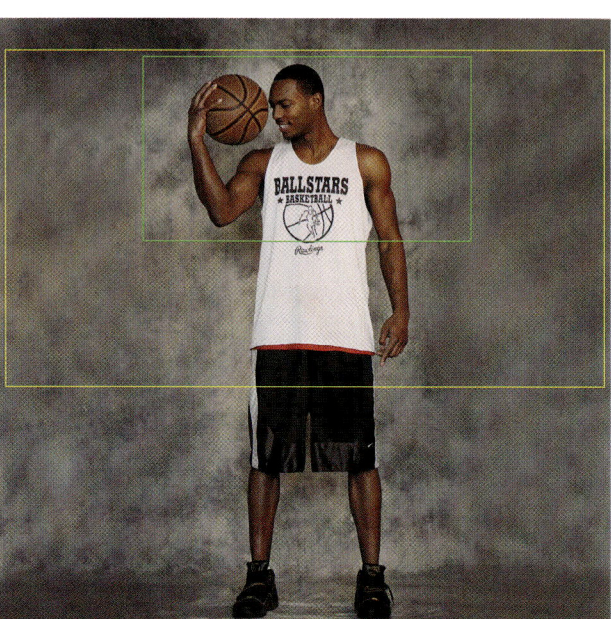

Figure 5.10

capture a vertical composition. Tricks like getting down on the floor and shooting up at your subject can exaggerate the perspective, but aren't a perfect solution.

Static shots where the camera is mounted on a tripod and everything's shot from the same distance are a recipe for dull videos. Try these tricks:

- **Establishing shot.** This composition, shown at left in Figure 5.11, establishes the scene and tells the viewer where the action is taking place.
- **Medium shot.** This shot is composed from about waist to headroom (some space above the subject's head). It's useful for providing variety from a series of close-ups and also makes for a useful first look at a speaker. (See Figure 5.11, right.)
- **Close-up.** The close-up, usually described as "from shirt pocket to head room," provides a good composition for someone talking directly to the camera. (See Figure 5.12, left.)
- **Extreme close-up.** This shot has been described as the "big talking face" shot. Styles and tastes change over the years and now the big talking face is much more commonly used (maybe people are better looking these days?) and so this view may be appropriate. (See Figure 5.12, right.)

- **"Two" shot.** A two shot shows a pair of subjects in one frame. They can be side by side or one in the foreground and one in the background. Subjects can be standing or seated. (See Figure 5.13, left.) A "three shot" is the same principle except that three people are in the frame.
- **Over-the-shoulder shot.** Long a tool of interview programs, the "over the shoulder shot" uses the rear of one person's head and shoulder to serve as a frame for the other person. This puts the viewer's perspective as that of the person facing away from the camera. (See Figure 5.13, right.)

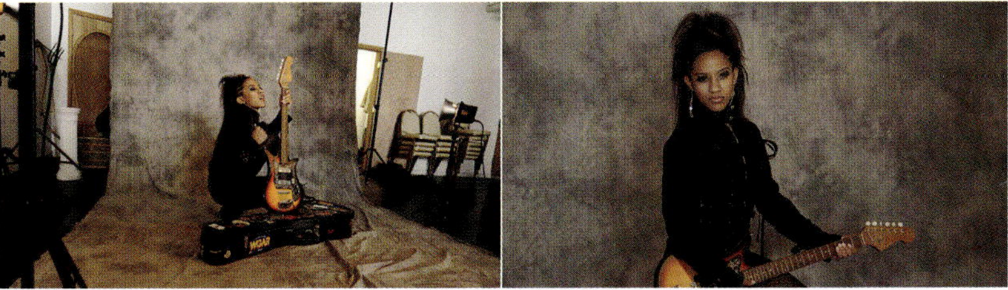

Figure 5.11

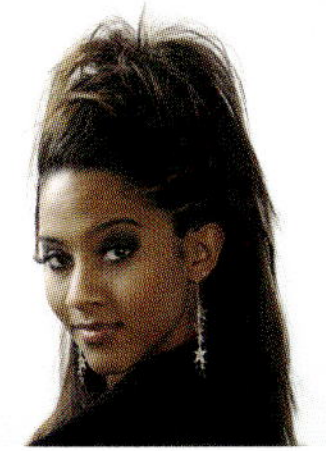

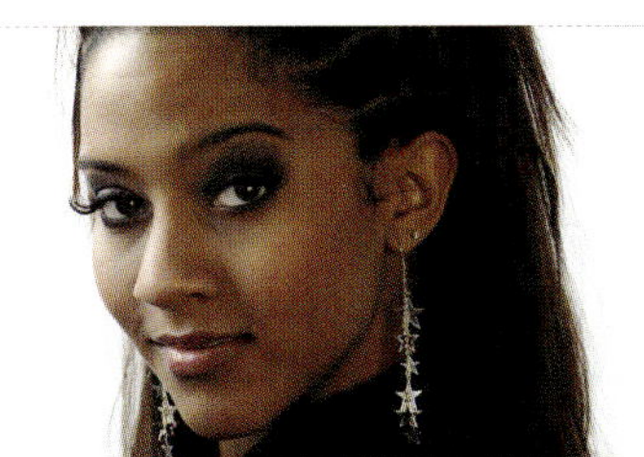

Figure 5.12

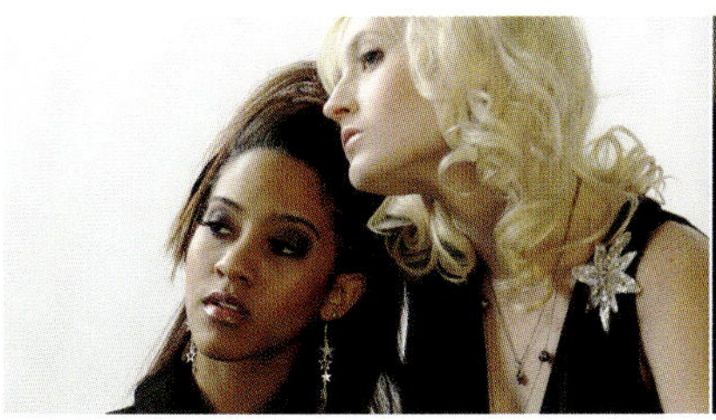

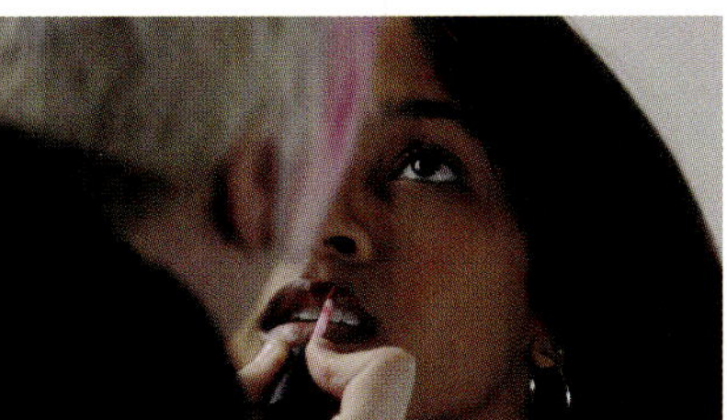

Figure 5.13

Chapter 6

Playback and Review

Point-and-shoot digital cameras offer much more than just the ability to see an image right after it's taken. The trend with digital cameras in general is to get rid of the "middle man;" in other words, the laptop or desktop computer.

Most mid-range point-and-shoot digital cameras provide a lot of options for viewing, editing, and processing your photos. Let's look at these three areas and see what we can expect.

Reviewing Images

Your camera offers a variety of playback options. Even the issue of simply viewing the image once it's been created is subject to user control. Some of your viewing options will include how long the image displays, what information it displays, and how many images are being displayed. You can also analyze your image and check the shooting settings to improve the next shot you take.

You can tweak what your camera displays during playback. Many cameras also give you the chance to mark (or "star") an image so you can designate it as a "keeper." Your camera should also give you the ability to "protect" a photo.

When you press the Playback button on your point-and-shoot camera, the most recently shot image appears on the screen. With most cameras, you can change the format/amount/type of information shown by pressing the Display/Info button. The screen may look something like Figure 6.1, in which the most recent image you took is shown with a minimal amount of information overlaid. As you continue to press the Display/Info button, the information display changes, perhaps switching to a full display (like the one shown in Figure 6.2), with a reduced-size thumbnail of the shot accompanied by lots of shooting data. You may be able to view a plain vanilla image (no distracting shooting data at all), or some other variation. When you press the Playback button, the format of that display will be the same as the last time you accessed the playback review function.

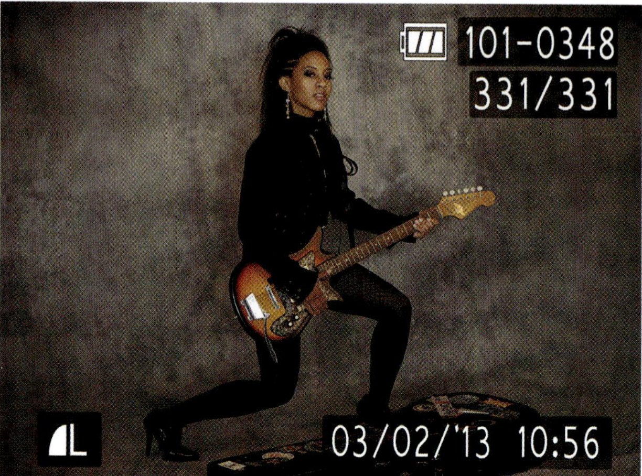

Figure 6.1
You can choose to review an image with only basic information overlaid...

As you review the image, you will also be able to zoom in to examine the picture, and scroll around within the frame to look at details up close. In any view, you can move on to the next picture or back to the previous one by pressing the left/right directional buttons or rotating a dial. Here are some of the types of information you can review:

- **Frame and folder number.** This is usually written something like 101-0348 (as in Figures 6.1 and 6.2), with the first number being the folder number and the second number the frame number.
- **Exposure information.** Just about every digital camera shows what your exposure settings were when you made the image. These might include exposure mode (P, or Program in Figure 6.2), shutter speed (in this case 1/125th second), ISO sensitivity setting (ISO 500 in the example), and f/stop (f/3.5 is shown). These are very useful bits of information because they help you make educated adjustments if the exposure seems off. You can change them before your next shot, perhaps adjusting the shutter speed, exposure mode, f/stop, or ISO setting.
- **Exposure compensation.** If you dialed in some exposure compensation, that information should be displayed as well. In Figure 6.2, exposure compensation is shown as 0.
- **White balance.** Displays the white balance setting used when the image was made, such as AWB (auto white balance) in Figure 6.2.
- **Resolution and image quality.** Your display will probably also show you what resolution setting your camera is using and what quality setting too, as shown in Figure 6.2. (10M, for 10 megabytes, and the L [Large] icon at lower left.)

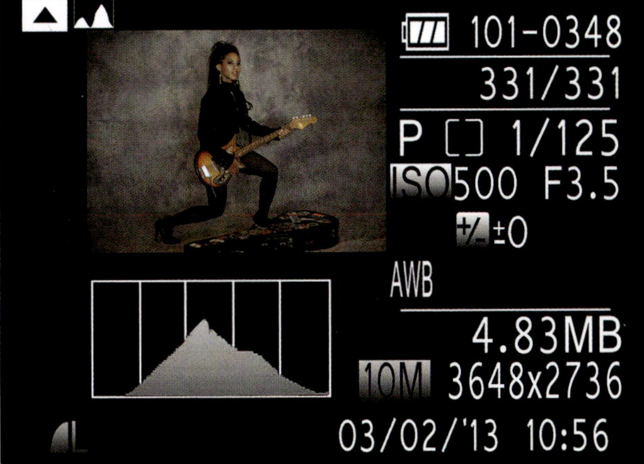

Figure 6.2
...or you can opt for a more comprehensive data display. Just press the Info or Display buttons to cycle through the options.

- **Flash information.** Was your flash on or off? If it was on, which particular flash setting was being used when you made the image? Many cameras will show that information in the review image.
- **Date and time display.** Shows when you created the image. Some cameras can even show all the images created on a particular day, using a calendar view.
- **Histogram.** This is a valuable tool for judging your exposure. A histogram is a graphical representation of how pixels are distributed through the image from darkest black to brightest white. Histograms are useful tools for judging image contrast and overall exposure.

Making Sense of Histograms

Some cameras can display a histogram graph while you are shooting (a "live histogram"), but virtually all have the ability to show you this useful chart in one of the review image data displays. The histogram is a more reliable indicator of exposure than the camera's LCD screen, which can often be misleading because of the limitations of the LCD display, and the lighting conditions under which you view it. The histogram itself never lies, and clearly provides useful information relating to your shot's exposure.

You'll need to build experience looking at histograms to become proficient in interpreting them. For example, you can evaluate a histogram to learn if your image is properly exposed. Tones at the left side of the graph represent darker tones in the image; those in the middle represent middle gray tones; and those at the right side show how many tones are lighter gray and white.

- **Underexposure.** Figure 6.3 shows an image that is underexposed. The mountain-shaped graph has all its values concentrated on the left, darker, side of the histogram. Indeed, the left side is "clipped off," meaning that some of the shadow information is entirely lost. There are no tones at all on the right side of the histogram, and, as you can see in the example, there are no true whites in the underexposed image. When you view a histogram of this sort, your response should be to add exposure. Dialing in some + (positive) exposure compensation is the easiest way to do that.
- **Overexposure.** When too much light reaches the sensor relative to the scene, the image is overexposed, as you can see in Figure 6.4. Now, the "mountain" has shifted to the far right, clipping off some of the white tones, leaving areas (such as the clouds) with no detail at all. There are no true blacks. To fix this image, you'd want to reduce exposure, usually with some – (negative) exposure compensation.
- **Correct exposure.** If you've done everything right, your picture will be properly exposed, as seen in Figure 6.5, and the histogram will show tones across the full expanse from black to white, with most of them (the peak of the mountain) in the middle tones.

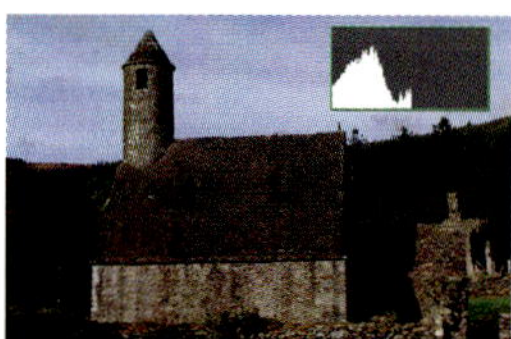

Figure 6.3 The histogram for an underexposed photograph.

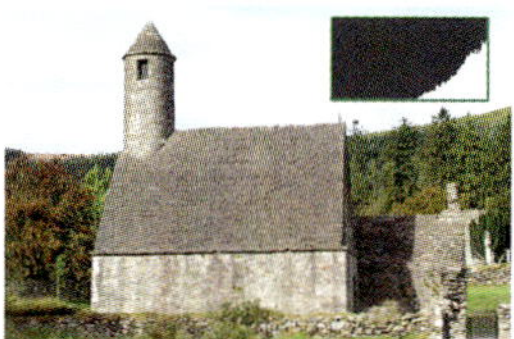

Figure 6.4 The histogram for an overexposed photograph.

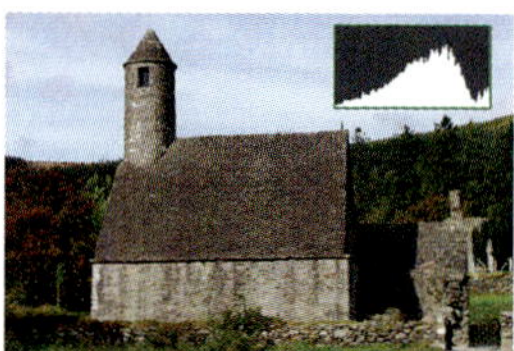

Figure 6.5 The histogram for a properly exposed photograph.

Zooming in on Your Image

Often, you'll want to zoom in on your image to take a closer look, perhaps to judge expressions or see if everyone in a group had their eyes open for the shot. Your camera provides the ability to zoom in and examine different parts of the image during review. Most cameras label the button or dial that lets you do this with a magnifying glass icon. Other cameras will rely on the zoom lever or input wheel (these are called a variety of names depending on the camera maker) for this function. Those with touch screens may let you zoom in by tapping on the screen in the area you want to examine.

Your camera may provide a thumbnail view with a navigation box that shows the zoomed area, or it may have a highlighted frame you can move around the

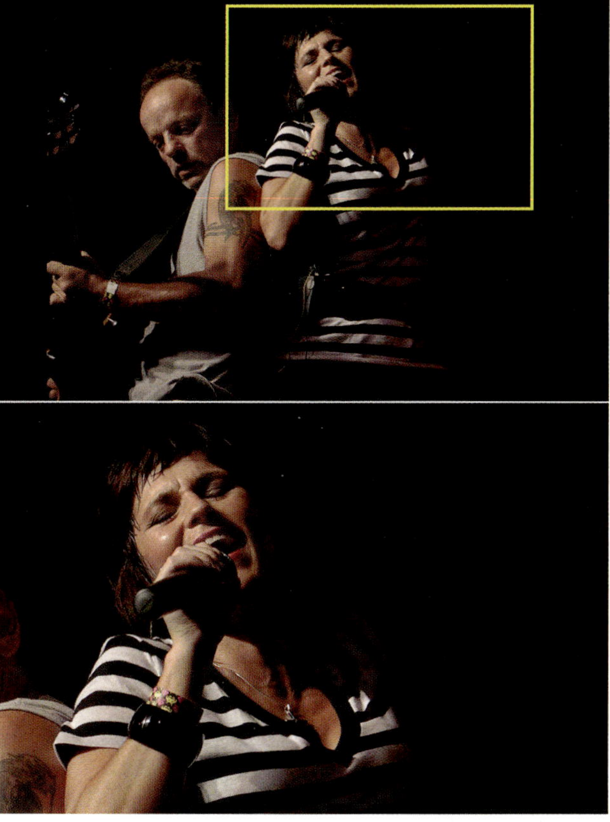

Figure 6.6
Zoom in on your image for a closer look.

screen with the directional buttons to zoom in. Figure 6.6 shows an overall image (top), and a zoomed-in version (bottom). Once you've zoomed in, you can usually maneuver around the image via either an input wheel or arrow keypad.

Playing Back Images on a Television Display

Most point-and-shoot cameras offer some way of connecting the camera to a television display. This is usually done in one of two ways, via an AV cable (most common and often provided with the camera) or HDMI (very common, too, but you have to buy your own HDMI cable).

The AV connection approach does a passable job. The cable will have three RCA plug connectors on the nether end, color-coded red/white (for left/right channels of stereo sound) and yellow (for composite video). Attach these to the matching red/white and yellow RCA jacks on your TV, VCR (remember those?), or other device. If your television or destination device does not have a video RCA connector, but does have an S-Video input, you can plug the yellow video output into a converter, like the one available from www.svideo-rca.com for about $14.

HDMI provides much higher quality playback, but requires the purchase of an appropriate cable (you need a mini HDMI to regular HDMI cable). Be careful if you decide to purchase one of these cables. Often the store makes more profit off of the cable than it does the big screen TV. Such cables are pushed for that reason and often things such as "gold contacts" are promoted for highest quality. Such enhancements were necessary for older cable technologies, but HDMI does not need such trimmings, as it is a digital technology that either works or does not work; there is no "degradation" caused by using a $5 cable instead of a $49 cable your big box store is pushing.

Once you're connected to a big-screen display, most digital cameras offer some sort of slideshow option you can use with your television to view your pictures. This tool lets you control timing and transitions as the slideshow plays on the TV screen. Some cameras can be remotely controlled by compatible television sets.

Editing

Your digital camera is designed to play back images for you so you can review them and then decide whether to keep or delete specific photos. Is it necessary to edit your photos in camera instead of on your computer? That's really something for you to decide. It's certainly faster and easier on a tablet, laptop, or desktop computer, but there can be times when you need to edit images immediately. For those times, editing in camera can be a workable idea. One thing to remember though is that it can be hard to accurately judge image quality just from the camera's LCD screen even with the ability to zoom in on areas of the image. It's best to exercise caution in deleting images that appear a touch soft or poorly exposed since it's possible an image-editing program may help you save those images.

Here are some of the editing tools your camera probably offers:

- **Image view.** When in full image view, your LCD shows one image. As described earlier, most cameras then offer the ability to zoom in as much as 10 times or greater so you can examine small areas of the photo in detail (and maneuver around the image as well). You can also zoom out to the point where your LCD shows multiple images, sometimes as many as 100 tiny thumbnails, or a calendar showing on what days pictures were shot, all on one screen.

- **Protect image.** Digital cameras give their operators the ability to protect images from accidental deletion. Most cameras will have you do this by pressing the Menu button and navigating to a "protect" option. Choosing the basic protect feature generally lets you view each image in full view and choose whether to protect the image (usually through a "Set" or "OK" button). The rare camera may actually have a protect button near the LCD screen, but this seems to be more common in micro four thirds and dSLR cameras. Be aware that even protected images can be wiped off the card when you reformat it. Protecting an image only protects it from erasing, not formatting.
- **Image deletion.** Most cameras use a trash can icon to mark the button you use to delete images. These are often multi-purpose buttons that serve a different function when your camera is in shooting mode. Some cameras incorporate the delete function into the playback menu and lack a physical trash button.
- **Image marking.** It's not unusual for a digital camera to offer some way of marking or rating an image. In some cases, your camera may offer you the ability to mark the image with from zero to five stars. Other cameras may help you designate a file for upload to a social networking or video sharing website. (See Figure 6.7.)
- **Image copying.** Some higher-end point-and-shoot cameras offer the ability to copy files from the camera's memory card to internal memory or internal memory to memory card.

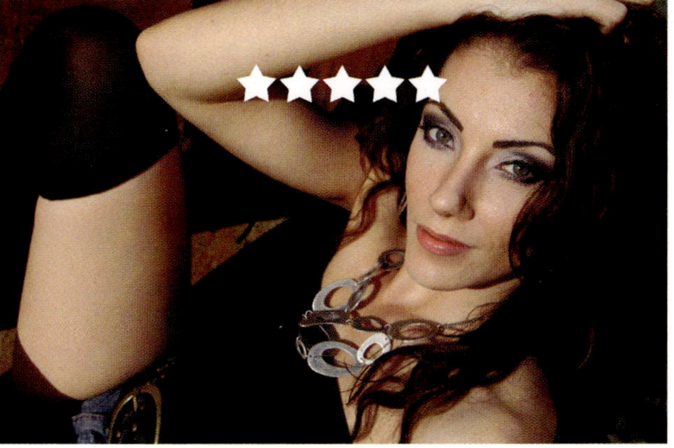

Figure 6.7
Rate your photos while they're still in your camera rather than waiting until you get home.

- **Image printing.** Marking images for printing is a common feature among point-and-shoot digital cameras and is one more way that your camera makes it possible to enjoy photography without having to get your home computer involved. (See Figure 6.8.) All you need is a compatible printer (any printer with a memory card reader built in and is Digital Print Order Format or "DPOF" capable) and you can print images without any other help. There are even small, portable printers that can travel with you if all you need are small prints.

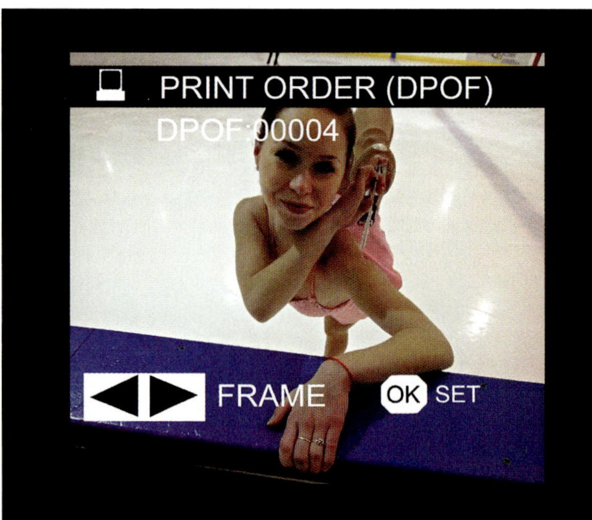

Figure 6.8
Choose which images you plan to print by using your camera's print selection capability and a DPOF (Digital Print Order Format) capable printer.

Image Processing

As digital sensors get better and better, and point-and-shoot cameras offer improved autofocus and exposure systems, the need for complicated workflow sequences in the digital darkroom have become less and less necessary, particularly for the typical photo enthusiast.

While many enthusiasts enjoy working in the digital darkroom and find great satisfaction in working to get the very best out of their images, many others prefer to devote their energies to creating images rather than processing them. The digital darkroom tools found in many point-and-shoot cameras make it possible to quickly and easily tweak an image while out in the field and prepare it for printing without ever having to set foot anywhere near a computer. When you think about how easy it is to find digital photo printing kiosks with editing capabilities at department stores and drug stores in most communities, this ability is a useful one.

In-camera editing options cover a variety of different digital darkroom areas, including image sizing and cropping, exposure and contrast correction, and retouching and color manipulation.

Image Sizing Options

Most point-and-shoot cameras at bare minimum offer the ability to crop or resize images (see Figure 6.9). Generally, these options are accessed through the camera's playback menu system. While photographers talk about "cropping" an image, your camera may call it "trimming" instead. Either way, the result is an image that's trimmed from the original image. Chances are good your camera will save a copy of the trimmed image while leaving the original intact, so if you have a full memory card, you may not be able to do this until you free up some space.

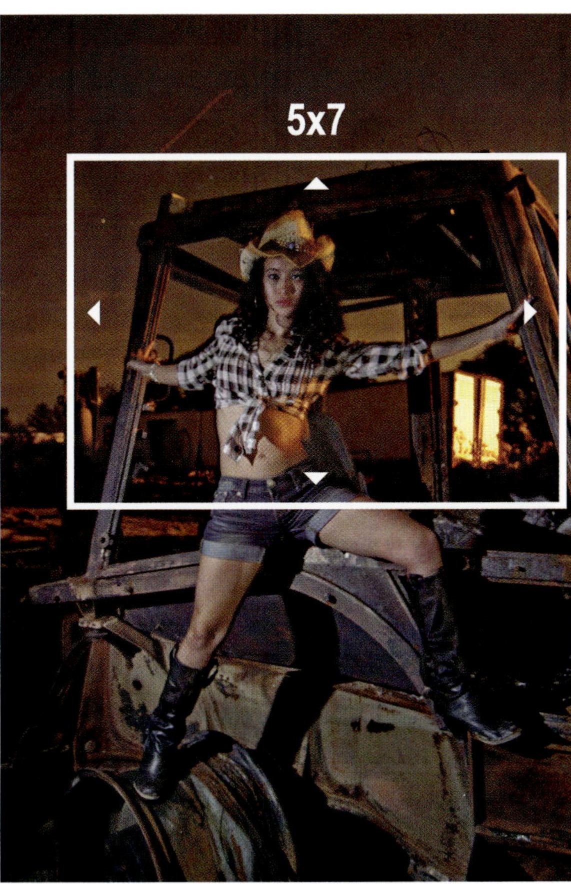

Figure 6.9
Many point-and-shoot cameras offer the ability to crop photos within the camera.

Remember, manipulating the image size doesn't improve resolution. If you crop/trim an image and then resize it larger, you may have some quality issues because the camera has to "invent" the extra pixels.

To find these options, set your camera to Playback mode, then press the Menu button. This should bring up the playback specific menu options. Once you've selected your processing choice, you can often designate more than one image for the effect (depending on your camera and the particular effect of course).

Exposure and Contrast Correction Options

Some form of exposure correction control should be an option for you depending on your camera. These will generally be pretty simple and heavily automated. Cameras that can shoot in RAW format tend to offer the greatest exposure and contrast correction options, whereas cameras that don't provide this option tend to have very limited capabilities in this area.

Your camera may offer a contrast or highlight/shadow adjustment. These are useful for dealing with images made in difficult lighting conditions. If you're not particularly comfortable in the digital darkroom or are in a hurry to print your images, these tools can give you satisfactory results if your original file is too far off.

RAW Files

If you have a point-and-shoot digital camera that can shoot in RAW mode, then you may have more in the way of editing options. Both the Canon G15 and Fuji X10 I'm working with for this book can shoot in RAW mode, but only the X10 appears to offer in-camera processing of RAW files. RAW mode is a powerful shooting option for when you need the best possible image. Because it creates larger files, it can also dramatically slow down your shooting rate, so it's not always the best choice for everyday use.

In-camera RAW processing can be an incredibly powerful tool if your camera offers that capability (see Figure 6.10). While it won't give you the same power as a computer-driven RAW converter (such as Adobe Photoshop's), it does give you the power to tweak your images when away from your computer. The advantage to RAW processing instead of JPEG processing is RAW processing is nondestructive. When you edit a JPEG file you're changing pixels, and if you do too much you can damage the image.

Let's take a look at the list of things some cameras can do to give us an example:

- **Reflect shooting condition.** Creates a JPEG of the RAW file exactly as the image was shot.
- **Push/pull processing.** Lets you adjust exposure up to one f/stop over or under exposure from the original image.
- **Dynamic range.** Gives you three choices regarding the dynamic range of the image (100%, 200%, and 400%).
- **Film simulation.** The X10 gives you eight different film simulation options (Provia, Velvia, Astia, Monochrome, Monochrome plus Yellow filter, Monochrome plus Red filter, Monochrome plus Green filter, Sepia).
- **White balance.** Change the white balance however you want (either via specific settings or by dialing in a specific color temperature in degrees Kelvin).
- **White balance shift.** Shift the image white balance by adjusting red/green and blue/yellow sliders.
- **Color.** Adjust image color via high to low options.
- **Sharpness.** Adjust image sharpness from hard to soft.
- **Highlight tone.** Adjust highlights from hard to soft.
- **Shadow tone.** Adjust shadows from hard to standard.
- **Noise Reduction.** Adjust image noise from high reduction to low reduction.
- **Color space.** Switch between sRGB and Adobe RGB as needed.

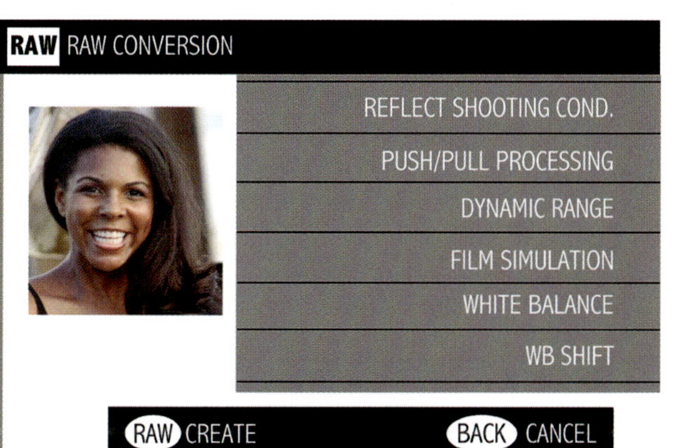

Figure 6.10
Some cameras offer a wide range of image processing options for their RAW files.

Retouching and Color Manipulation Options

Red-eye correction is one retouching option the vast majority of point-and-shoot cameras offer. Generally, once you select this option, the camera does the work for you, recognizing the red-eye and fixing it. Of course, one potential problem is that if the subject is wearing a similar shade of red clothing, the camera may try to "fix" that too.

Color manipulation is another color option found in many cameras. Often this manipulation has to do with changing the color of the image to reflect a film type or classic photo effect such as Sepia toning or some version of black-and-white image or making colors more vivid or saturated. While these options sound like some of those mentioned in the previous section, it's important to understand that unlike the RAW conversion manipulations, these options can degrade the quality of the image. It's not likely to be a big deal in most cases unless you do additional manipulations at some other stage of the process. It's the cumulative effect of multiple edits that usually results in noticeable image degradation.

Printing Images

It's interesting to see how digital photography has produced something of a change in the way photo enthusiasts display and share their photographs. In the past, photographers had prints made from their negatives and either made enlargements for hanging on their walls or prints to display in photo albums. Although many of us still do that, newer technologies have given us other options. Digital photo frames let us display our photos without having to get them printed, and photobooks let us replace clunky photo albums with good-looking bound volumes benefitting from professional layout and design templates that help even the novice produce a good-looking book of their images.

A common feature on many point-and-shoot digital cameras helps you choose and mark images for inclusion in photobooks. In some cases, you can even designate a cover photo and choose which images are used and what order they're used in. You can then use the camera's accompanying software to upload your photobook to one of the online services that offer this product.

Your camera will also let you select and mark images for printing with a DPOF (Digital Print Order Format) capable printer. You can even designate the number of prints to be made from each file. Once done, just remove the memory card from your camera and insert it in the memory card slot on the printer. Follow your printer's instructions to print your images. Or, you can take the card to a photo dealer or print it yourself at a kiosk.

Wi-Fi and Geotagging

These days, Wi-Fi and GPS capabilities work together with your point-and-shoot camera in interesting new ways. Some cameras have wireless or GPS capabilities built-in. Others lack those features, but are compatible with add-ons, such as the Eye-Fi SD memory card, which contains its own Wi-Fi communications hardware.

Wireless capabilities allow you to upload photos directly from your point-and-shoot camera to your computer at home or in your studio, or, through a hotspot at your hotel or coffee shop back to your home computer or to a photo-sharing service like Facebook or Flickr. A special Wi-Fi-enabled memory card that you slip in the SD slot of your camera performs the magic. GPS capabilities—built right into some of those Wi-Fi cards—allow you to mark your photographs with location information, so you don't have to guess where a picture was taken.

Both capabilities are very cool. Wi-Fi uploads can provide instant backup of important shots and sharing. Geotagging is most important as a way to associate the geographical location where the photographer was when a picture was taken, with the actual photograph itself. It can be done with the location-mapping capabilities of the Wi-Fi card, or through add-on devices that third parties make available for your point-and-shoot.

Geotagging can also be done by attaching geographic information to the photo after it's already been taken. This is often done with online sharing services, such as Flickr, which allow you to associate your uploaded photographs with a map, city, street address, or postal code. When properly geotagged and uploaded to sites like Flickr, users can browse through your photos using a map, find pictures you've taken in a given area, or even search through photos taken at the same location by other users.

Each Eye-Fi card (www.eye-fi) is an SDHC memory card with a wireless transmitter built in. You insert it in your camera just as with any ordinary card, and then specify which networks to use. You can add as many as 32 different networks. The next time your camera is on within range of a specified network, your photos and videos can be uploaded to your computer and/or to your favorite sharing site. During setup, you can customize where you want your images uploaded. The Eye-Fi card will only send them to the computer and to the sharing site you choose.

Uploads over these networks can go to your own destinations or to any of 25 popular sharing websites, including Flickr, Facebook, Costco, Adorama, Smugmug, YouTube, Shutterfly, or Walmart. Online Sharing is included as a lifetime, unlimited service with all Pro X2 cards. Although the Eye-Fi card does not have a GPS receiver, it uses information from connected Wi-Fi networks to determine the current location, and embeds that in the image files stored on the card.

When uploading to online sites, you can specify not just where your images are sent, but how they are organized, by specifying preset album names, tags, descriptions, and even privacy preferences on certain sharing sites. (You should be cautious about sharing your location when using social media sites.) Some Eye-Fi cards also include a geotagging service, which help you view uploaded photos on a map, and sort them by location. Eye-Fi's geotagging uses Wi-Fi Positioning System (WPS) technology. Using built-in Wi-Fi, the Eye-Fi card senses surrounding Wi-Fi networks as you take pictures. When photos are uploaded, the Eye-Fi service then adds the geotags to your photos. You don't need to have the password or a subscription for the Wi-Fi networks the card accesses; it can grab the location information directly without the need to "log in." You don't need to set up or control the Eye-Fi card from your camera. Software on your computer manages all the parameters.

If you frequently travel outside the range of your home (or business) Wi-Fi network, an optional service called Hotspot Access is available, allowing you to connect to any AT&T Wi-Fi hotspot in the USA. In addition, you can use your own Wi-Fi accounts from commercial network providers, your city, even organizations you belong to such as your university.

The card has another interesting feature called Endless Memory. When pictures have been safely uploaded to an external site, the card can be set to automatically erase the oldest images to free up space for new pictures. You choose the threshold where the card starts zapping your old pictures to make room.

Chapter 7

Shooting Tips

Today's point-and-shoot digital cameras are marvels of technology, but we don't want to lose sight of what's important—creating memorable images, not owning the fanciest technology. In this section we're going to look at techniques for creating better photos.

As digital cameras have gotten smarter, the content needed for sections such as this one has diminished. Pre-programmed exposure and white balance modes designed to deal with problematic exposure conditions have made it easier for photo enthusiasts to be more successful in their image making. Still, there are some things that just can't be solved by a computer program.

Next, we'll look at tips and tricks that can help you improve the quality of your photos.

Lighting Tricks

It's hard to overstate the importance of light for good photography. Successful lighting is much more difficult than just having enough light for a proper exposure.

"Good" lighting can make our photos better in many ways. It can emphasize what's important in the image, add depth and dimension, and it can create a mood. It can reveal detail or soften harsh wrinkles and blemishes. Light can also add color and tone to a photograph, making it more inspiring or more threatening.

In the quest for effective lighting, pro photographers invest thousands of dollars in lighting and flash equipment. If you're reading this book and thinking you can't afford to buy expensive equipment, and you don't want to have to lug it around with you, you're going to need a more practical set of solutions for your photography.

The good news is that there are things you can do to dramatically improve the lighting in your photography, and without spending much or any money on accessories. We're going to look at some options ranging from zero cost to just a few dollars (and often "do it yourself" options).

When we talk about light, there are several important considerations. These include quantity, quality, color, and direction. We can use these independently or in combination to make better photos.

Light Quantity

Inexperienced photographers often concentrate on whether they have "enough" light for a properly exposed image. While this is an important starting point, the methods they employ are often not the best options. For example, the tiny built-in flash unit on a point-and-shoot camera is usually a very poor choice for increasing light on your subject. This light isn't very powerful; it tends to be harsh and unflattering and because it is located so close to the lens, it usually causes red-eye, that strange red glow in your subject's eyes.

Before resorting to using the built-in flash, you should consider other options. Often you'll get better and more creative lighting by raising window shades or blinds, turning on more room lights, or moving a lamp or two closer to your subject. You can also move your subject closer to the main light source. One other consideration is reflective surfaces. If you can work in a room with white walls, or bring in mirrors, these can "bounce" light back onto your subject, providing more even illumination. I often shoot ice hockey and figure skating. It's fascinating how even the lighting is in ice rinks simply because light is bouncing up off the ice and filling in shadow areas. It's a very soft, even lighting (see Figure 7.1).

Even pulling out the work lights from your garage can do the trick (or buying an inexpensive set for your photography). You can use them to direct additional light on the scene, or, extend the tripod as high as it will go, point the lights up at the ceiling (into a corner works really well), and bounce the light off the ceiling to flood the room with soft even lighting. Just be aware that the light will pick up the color of the ceiling.

Light Quality

Light can be either "hard" or "soft." Each has its own way of affecting how your photos look, and each can be a problem when used incorrectly. The trick is to understand whether your image lends itself to contrasty, detail enhancing hard light, or would benefit more from soft, diffuse illumination.

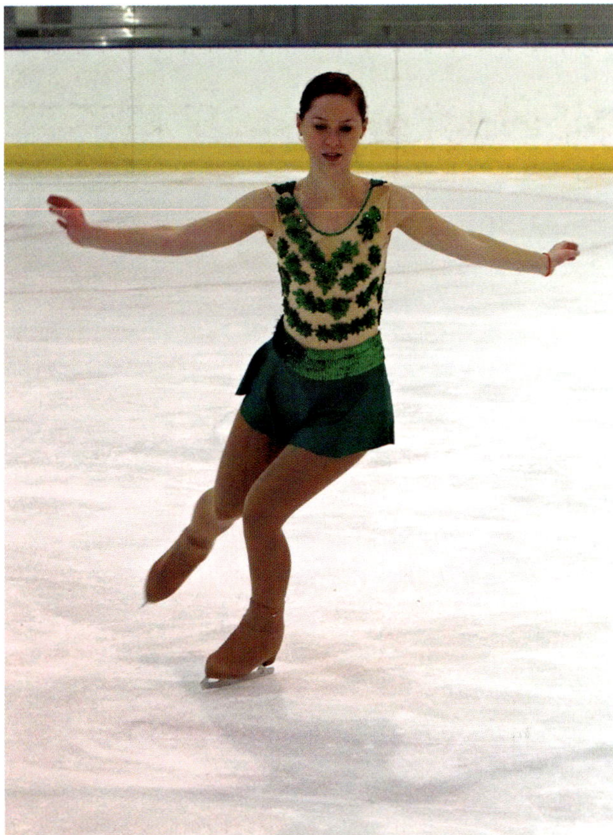

Figure 7.1
When light falls on a reflective surface such as ice it can "bounce" the light back on to your subject.

Hard Light

This is a small (relative to the subject), concentrated light source. Any relatively small light source placed close to the subject will produce a hard light. Even our massive sun is a relatively small light source and produces a hard light.

Hard light is great for showing detail. This is super for photographing objects or textures, but not so good for photographing people. Hard light shows the wrinkles, blemishes, and skin flaws most of us prefer to hide; hard lighting is seldom appropriate for portraiture (see Figure 7.2).

- **Work lights.** As mentioned earlier, work lights are good for showing detail, particularly for something like macro photography. While the packaged kits are nice and usually include light stands, if you're on a tight budget, you can find inexpensive work lights that clamp to chairs, poles, or doors.

- **Auto headlights.** In a pinch your car's headlights can produce a lot of light. While this light is relatively portable (so long as there's a road around at least), it can be hard to maneuver them exactly where you need them. Still, they do produce a lot of light.
- **Portable spotlights.** These are portable and put out a good amount of light. They can also be very useful for "painting with light," a technique that involves putting your camera on a stable surface, setting it for a long exposure (at night or in a dark room), and moving the spotlight's illumination over the surface to "paint" the object with light to give it sufficient exposure.
- **Light sticks/Flashlights/LED lights.** There are a wide variety of small, portable lights you can use to be more creative in your photography. Depending on your subject, these can be used for direct lighting or in a painting with light image.

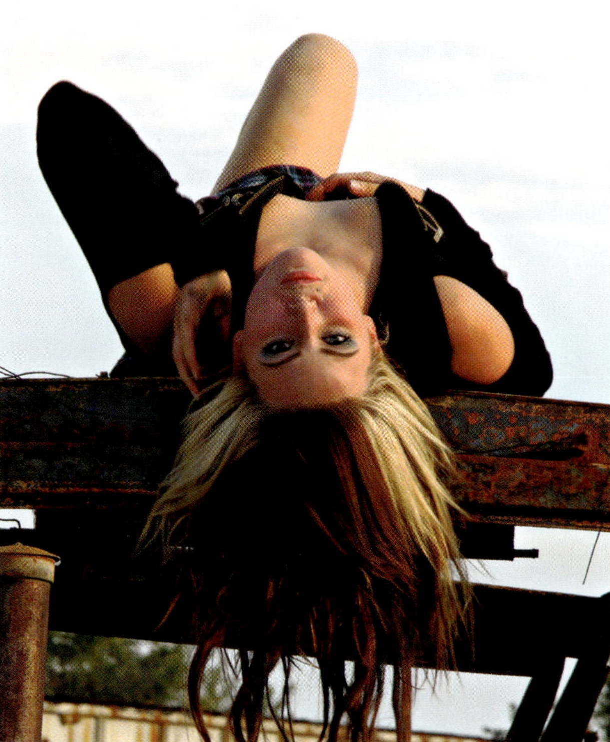

Figure 7.2
While great for showing detail, "hard" light is not ideal for portraiture.

- **Portable flash units.** If you're using a slow enough shutter speed (or the manual open/manual close "Bulb" setting if your camera has one), you can manually trigger just about any portable flash unit (via the test button on the flash). Just press the shutter button, point the flash, and press the test button (before the shutter closes).
- **Video lights.** You know those little continuous lights they sell for video camcorders? Well, they work just fine on a point-and-shoot camera, especially if the camera has a hot shoe. Even if it doesn't, you can hold the light in your hand, place it on a table, or ask someone else to hold it. These lights are inexpensive (sometimes as little as $35), small, and lightweight. They don't put out a lot of light, but if you can get them close to your subject, they provide a useful amount of illumination. Bigger video lights can offer more output, which means their illumination will reach farther into the background. However, a large light may throw off the balance of the camera/light combination because many of these lamps are actually larger than the camera. One added bonus is that you can use the video light for recording video with your point-and-shoot camera too. Since many good point-and-shoot digital cameras can record HD-quality video, this can be a worthwhile investment (see Figure 7.3).

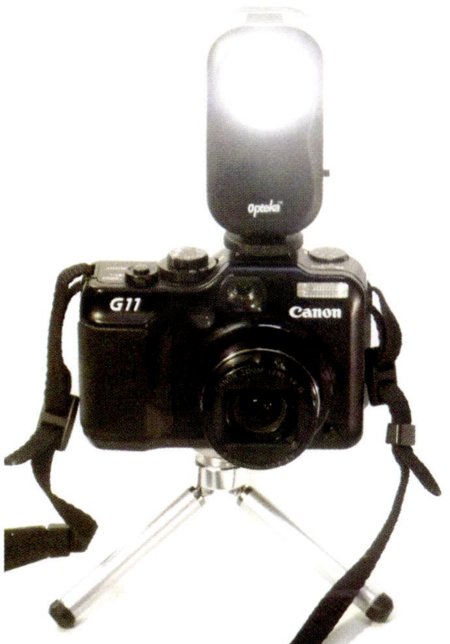

Figure 7.3
LED video lights provide some extra illumination for capturing movies in dim light.

Soft Light

When the light source is big in relation to the subject, and its light spreads out nice and wide, it softens and becomes gentler. Hard light, because it's so directional, creates shadows (which help make detail stand out) that emphasize wrinkles and blemishes. Because light from a soft light source is spread out, it bounces off surfaces in all directions, creating a more even lighting. Professional shooters use light modifiers to soften light when shooting portraits or any time they want a softer light. These light modifiers diffuse (spread) and soften the light either by bouncing the light into a reflective surface on something like an umbrella or through a soft box, which causes the light to spread and sends it through a frosted white material to diffuse it even more.

Such tools aren't really practical for photo enthusiasts who just want to take better photos with their point-and-shoot cameras. While it is possible to set up a portable photo studio (using portable flash units and light modifiers designed to work on them), that's something most hobbyists have no interest in doing. It kind of defeats the purpose of carrying a small and light camera if you have to carry a bunch of extra gear. Instead, we need to take advantage of the resources that might be available on-site.

"Bouncing Light"

One thing to keep in mind about the hard light/soft light issue is that any light source can be made softer. Go back to our definition of hard light being a relatively small light source placed close to the subject. "Soft" light on the other hand is light that has been spread out, creating a relatively large light source.

I keep using some version of the word "relative" when describing the size of the light source. This is because it's not the actual size of the light source, it's the relative size that counts. The sun is an immense light source, but it's also so far away it's relatively tiny compared to our subject. A pencil flashlight is a physically small light source, but a relatively large one if you're positioning it just above a fruit fly. In this case it becomes a "soft" light even though it is a physically small and direct light.

Any "hard" light source can be softened by finding a way to spread the light pattern so the size of the light source relative to your subject is increased. "Bouncing" light means instead of pointing the light at your subject, you point it in the direction of a reflective surface that spreads the light out and returns it to your subject. More often than not that means the nearest wall, but there are other things that work well. Mirrors actually return more light than walls do, although the wall will soften (diffuse) the light more than the mirror will. One thing to bear in mind though is that directing the light toward a wall increases the distance the light has to travel, reducing the power of the light.

This means that every time you double the distance the light has to travel, you reduce its power by a factor of four.

Another method of softening light is to "diffuse" it. Do this by shining the light through a material that causes the light to spread. This in effect, can turn a small light source into a larger one. This works best when there's a little space between the light source and the diffusion material. A simple example of a homemade diffuser would be to take a wooden screen and stretch a white pillowcase over it. Place the light about a foot away from the homemade diffuser and your hard light will be softer.

"Diffused" light is very flattering and often used in portraiture because of its pleasing results (see Figure 7.4).

- **Work Lights.** A set of work lights raised up on their light stands can bounce a lot of light off a wall, ceiling, or corner and turn them into a soft, effective, and versatile light source.
- **Lamps.** You can use a basic household lamp to bring additional light into a scene. Table or floor lamps use the same principle as discussed in the last section; they use a diffusion material between the light and the user. Lampshades soften light nicely. You can vary the power of the light by moving it closer or farther from your subject. Halogen lamps that direct light upward to the ceiling are doing their own form of bounce lighting.

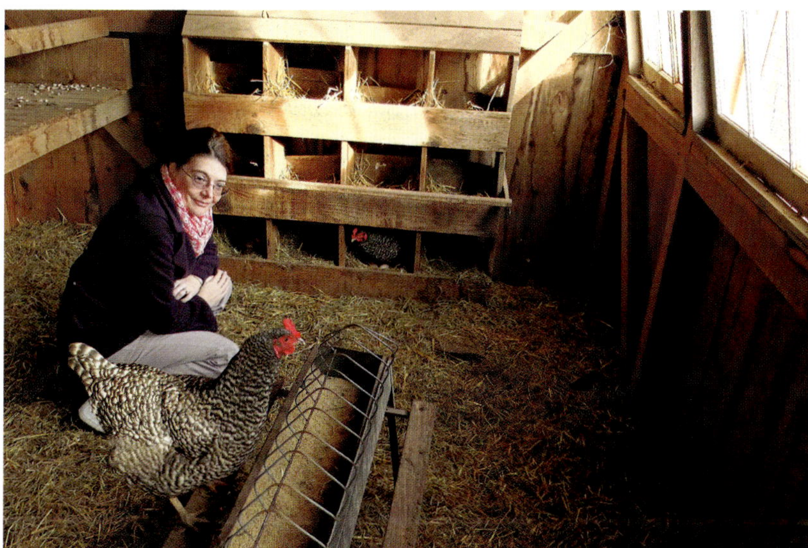

Figure 7.4 Light can be diffused through a window shade, lampshade, or some other material. The resulting light can make for beautiful portraits.

- **Window light.** Light streaming through a screened window is a beautiful diffuse light that can create a soft lovely light. Position your subject in that light, expose for the highlight on their window side cheek, and fire away.
- **Pop-up flash light modifier.** If your camera has a pop-up flash, then it may be possible to attach a small light modifier to either diffuse or bounce the light and soften it. Usually the diffuser is a better choice since the light from the pop-up flash isn't very powerful to begin with. Redirecting its light (so it can bounce off a wall or ceiling) ends up increasing the distance that light has to travel to the point where it's been weakened considerably. While firing the flash through a diffuser also reduces light output, it will still most likely be stronger than light bounced off a ceiling.

Available Light

Available or *existing* light is just what it sounds like—light coming from room lights, streetlights, sunlight, and other light sources (even automobile lights). This light can be strong enough to give us good exposures, but if we learn to understand how to use it more creatively, it can also help us produce more beautiful images.

One classic example is the window-lit portrait. This shot is pretty easy to create, and if done properly, produces a beautifully and dramatically lit photograph. Position your subject so the light that is streaming through a window lights her from the side. You can make it more dramatic by dimming or turning off room lights so the window light is the only light source, or you can experiment by using room lights to add a little light to the shadow side of the subject. Either way, the result is an image that's far more interesting than any shot made with a built-in flash (see Figure 7.5).

Filters and Digital Cameras

Filters are pieces of glass or resin that fit over your lens to change the image striking your lens in some way. Their importance has declined in the digital era, particularly since digital cameras can replicate many of the things conventional filters used to do and software programs such as Photoshop Elements can cover others.

While that's mostly true, there are still things that are only possible with conventional filters or easier to accomplish than trying to do so during the digital darkroom process. Certain filters are still quite handy and worth owning. The problem with many point-and-shoot cameras is that their lenses aren't designed to accept filters. The good news is some camera makers offer adapters to attach

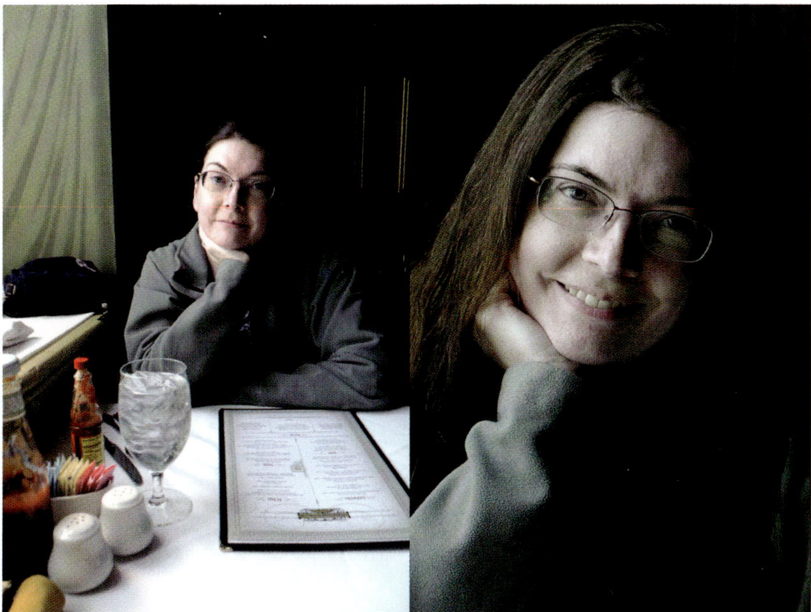

Figure 7.5 Window light can be used to create dramatic and romantic portraits.

a filter to your camera. Cokin, a maker of rectangular resin filters offers an adapter for its filters, which mounts via the camera's tripod socket (you can find the Cokin adapters on eBay for less than $10).

There are lots of filters on the market, many of which date back before the latest era of digital cameras. Not all of them are worth spending money on. Here's a rundown of some of the choices available, what they're good for, and whether you might be interested in them:

- **Polarizing filter.** The tried and true polarizing filter has been around for decades and is still a versatile and valuable addition to any photographic arsenal. These filters can improve images in several ways. They can increase contrast with color images and most importantly, can reduce or eliminate non-metallic reflections. They're great after a rainstorm (all those water droplets act as mini mirrors) or when trying to shoot through glass, such as when you're visiting an aquarium. Variations of this filter may include a warming effect so you don't have to stack multiple filters. You want a circular polarizer for cameras with autofocus systems, not linear polarizers (see Figure 7.6).

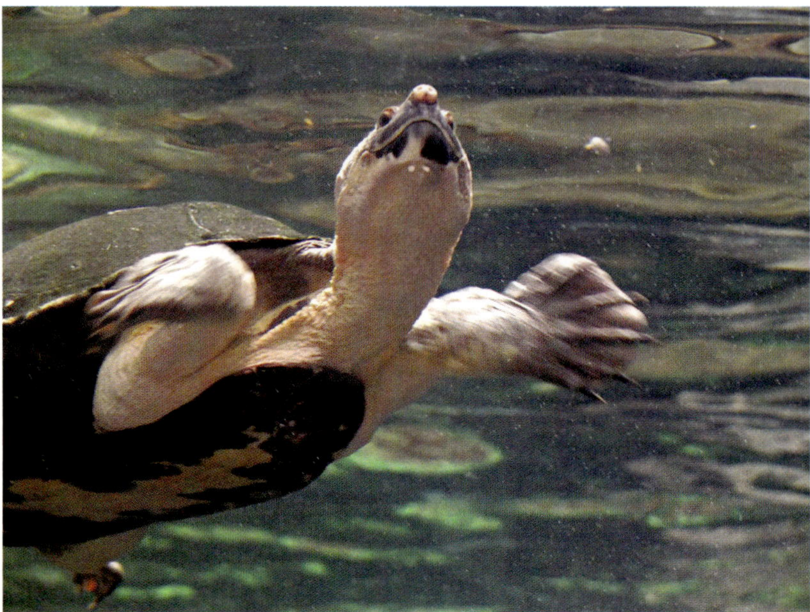

Figure 7.6 Shooting a turtle in an aquarium. A polarizing filter helped eliminate reflections in the glass.

- **Soft focus filter.** These diffusing filters are useful in glamour and portrait photography and especially creative photographers can often find ways to apply them creatively for other situations where a soft image is desirable.
- **Neutral density/Graduated neutral density.** A neutral density filter is designed to reduce the amount of light reaching the sensor, allowing you to use longer shutter speeds. It's not unusual for a point-and-shoot camera to have a built-in "ND" filter option, so add-on versions of these filters may not be necessary. There is a variation of this filter though that can be a good investment. A graduated neutral density filter is designed to reduce light passing through one-half of the filter, then gradually fading to clear to admit all the light. These filters are useful when one part of the scene is considerably brighter than another. Landscape photographers often use these filters to correct when skies are considerably brighter than the landscape by reducing the light reaching the sensor from the upper half of the scene only.

- **Star filter.** These filters turn lights into stars. This happens because these filters have a crosshatch pattern etched into them. You can get the same effect by stretching a black nylon stocking over your lens or holding a piece of window screen in front of it.
- **Sunset filter.** This filter gradually goes from a rich orange-yellow to a much lighter yellow-orange in order to mimic the light from a sunrise or sunset. While it does a reasonably good job, you can create the same effect on your home computer fairly easily.
- **Close-up filters/Macro lenses.** These are often thought of as filters since they screw into the lens filter thread, but from a technical standpoint they're actually considered lenses. Filters are pieces of flat glass, while lenses are pieces of concave glass with one or more elements.
- **Other filters.** There are a lot of other types of filters on the market, but odds are they'll offer little value to the hobbyist and probably aren't worth the trouble of carrying around.

So just how important are filters for a point-and-shoot camera user? For most shooters I'd say not particularly. However, I would suggest buying the polarizing filter, which can solve problems and improve photos considerably.

The others listed above can be helpful, but if you're thinking it's just something else you have to carry around and keep track of and it's not worth the hassle, I can't disagree with you. Chances are you chose a point-and-shoot camera because you want to keep things simple and easy. That's fine; you can still get great pictures without filters.

Video

Today's point-and-shoot cameras are capable of stunning video quality. Unfortunately, great technical quality alone isn't enough. In observing amateur videos on the web, it's easy to see the same basic problems cropping up over and over.

There are certain simple things you can do to make your videos better. At the very top of your list should be keeping your camera steady. Even with the image stabilization most good point-and-shoot cameras offer, it's hard to hold a camera steady enough for good quality video.

While a tripod is the likely answer, there are other solutions that don't require lugging more gear. Any reasonably level, solid platform can serve as a place to rest your camera so that it creates steadier video. And unlike with still photographs, there's no need to worry about shooting the occasional vertical. Videos should be shot horizontally since the usual displays for these graphics are horizontally oriented.

Another tip for better video is to improve your lighting. The video light mentioned earlier in this chapter is a great tool. Other options include turning on more room lights or setting up work lights out of camera view.

Audio

Poor audio quality is one of the biggest issues with digital video, and there are limits to what you can do with a point-and-shoot camera to improve it. Very few inexpensive point-and-shoot cameras can take an external microphone. The best you can usually hope for is that your camera has a built-in stereo microphone of decent quality.

Try to get your camera closer to the scene so the microphone picks up more of your subject's voice than the background noises. Turn off all fans and any other machinery or noise making devices no matter how little noise they seem to make, and reduce the amount of noise-inducing zooming and focusing you do. Our ears automatically filter out background noises; microphones don't.

Index

A

B

C

D

E

F

J

L

M

Q

R

S

T